CHICAGO
DAYS

HOBOKEN
NIGHTS

BOOKS BY DANIEL PINKWATER

Daniel Pinkwater

CHICAGO
DAYS

HOBOKEN
NIGHTS

ADDISON-WESLEY PUBLISHING COMPANY

Reading, Massachusetts   Menlo Park, California   New York
Don Mills, Ontario   Wokingham, England   Amsterdam   Bonn
Sydney   Singapore   Tokyo   Madrid   San Juan
Paris   Seoul   Milan   Mexico City   Taipei

*In memory of David Nyvall, who asked, ''Do you
know what you're doing?''*

And to my mother, who said, ''Everybody has a family.''

Many of the designations used by manufacturers and sellers to distinguish
their products are claimed as trademarks. Where those designations appear in
this book and Addison-Wesley was aware of a trademark claim, the
designations have been printed in initial capital letters (i.e., Pepsi Cola).

Library of Congress Cataloging-in-Publication Data

Pinkwater, Daniel Manus, 1941–
Chicago days/Hoboken nights / Daniel Pinkwater.
p.   cm.
ISBN 0-201-52359-0
ISBN 0-201-63225-X (pbk.)
I. Title.
PS3566.I526C48   1991
813'.54—dc20   91-19573
CIP

Copyright © 1991 by Daniel Pinkwater

Jacket design by absolute design
Text design by Dede Cummings
Set in 11-point Meridien by Pagesetters, Inc.
1   2   3   4   5   6   7   8   9-MW-95949392
First printing, September 1991
First paperback printing, August 1992

CONTENTS

❧ ❧ ❧

ACKNOWLEDGMENTS

AMONG the good-natured, hard-working, under-paid, and (well, yes, they actually are) dedicated people who work on "All Things Considered," I want to offer special thanks to Bob Boilen and Margaret Low Smith. My editor on this project was Jane Isay, who, by the expedients of feeding me small pieces of cooked liver and not making any sudden moves, was able to overcome decades of negative experience and actually get me to trust her.

PREFACE

THIS book, like *Fish Whistle*, which preceded it, is a collection of short pieces, mostly commentaries originally aired on National Public Radio's "All Things Considered." *Fish Whistle* consisted of a random assortment of pieces from the first two years of that pleasant association. The present volume contains a selection from years three and four and also turns out to be a fragmentary autobiography. I'm a little surprised by this—I hadn't intended to write one. I guess I got so comfortable with my audience that I didn't mind revealing a whole lot about my own life, something I never do when I write fiction.

Professional as it may be, there's a home-town radio aspect to NPR that promotes a kind of intimacy and familiarity. People listen in their cars and while preparing the evening meal and feel easy about communicating with the fellow who's just been talking to them, telling a story about school days or an eccentric relative.

Frequently a listener will feel prompted to send me a story of his or her own. Theirs are generally superior to mine, which suggests that the reason I'm the guy on the radio may be that other people have better things to do.

One family wrote that they regard me as an old friend who doesn't drop by the house as often as he used to (but is welcome just the same). Listeners phone me at home almost every week. In four years I have spoken to only one obnoxious son of a bitch—and even he had some pretty good points to make.

Pinkwater's first rule of writing is to respect the reader. This means making all clear, keeping it entertaining, not showing off gratuitously, and not kissing the reader's intellectual ass. (That last part of the rule, I've always thought, might be the reason I don't get much play from the more illuminated literary types, *entre nous savants*). What I'm trying to get at is that the pieces in this book were written for an audience that's easy to respect—and even like.

If in reading these you get the impression that I've been having a good time, you'll be right. I wish you the same.

CHICAGO
DAYS

IF you're a writer, one of the things you get to do is go around and give talks. The reason for this eludes me. People have the idea that if someone is able to write a story, sitting in front of a typewriter or a computer, with all the time in the world, and a dictionary and a thesaurus at hand—that person must be smart and have things to say worth listening to.

I occasionally go around and give talks myself. Why do I do it? Well, they pay me. And sometimes I get to go someplace nice—like Flagstaff, Arizona—I really liked it there.

The first time I ever took a trip as an author it was to Rochester, New York. The children's librarians of the county invited me to come and talk to them. They paid me two hundred dollars, my train fare, my motel room, and all the chop suey I could eat.

Now it so happened that Rochester was a city I'd always wanted to visit. You see, there's a fat man's clothing factory there, and I hoped to buy some stuff wholesale.

When you're a fat guy you can't just walk into Penney's and buy a sport jacket and a pair of stone-washed jeans. Most of the time, you're obliged to order stuff out of catalogs for ''Big and Tall Men.'' These are the last sources on earth for leisure suits, white plastic belts, and Hawaiian motif boxer shorts. And the prices are steep. It costs me a pretty good dollar to cover myself in polyester.

So I readily accepted the gig in Rochester, and as soon as I got finished boring everybody, I went hotfoot to the Mega-Man clothing factory.

They were real nice to me. Knew who I was. They remembered me for my tasteful orders of Filipino Mabuhey shirts in pastel colors, and pleated plaid dacron trousers with the elastic waist.

A fellow from the office, name of Bill, took me upstairs to the sample room.

"Everything in here is slightly irregular, or stuff we decided not to make, or special orders that never got delivered. Tell me what you like, and I'll make you a nice price," he said.

It was double-extra-large heaven. I got a half-dozen sport shirts at five dollars apiece, a really nice windbreaker—also five dollars—two pairs of pants and a belt.

"Pinky, can you use a few cowboy suits?" Bill asked me.

"Cowboy suits?"

Bill indicated a row of garments covered by plastic bags, hanging from a pipe near the ceiling. There must have been a half-dozen—all different colors.

"We made them up for some cowboy singer, but he died or went broke, or lost weight. They're real nice—and they're in your size."

They were real nice. They had fringes, and embroidered arrowheads, and bucking broncos, and horseshoes.

"Take 'em all for fifty bucks, Pinky," Bill said.

"Well . . . I don't know."

"They're complete. Pants and jacket, cowboy shirt—even neckties. All you'll need is boots, a hat, and cowboy underwear."

I could get one of those hats with the big feather in front, I thought. Maybe spurs. God—I'd look good.

"Want me to put 'em in a box?"

I could start hanging out in those cowboy bars that were popular in Long Island, where I lived then. I could start dipping snuff. Maybe I'd try riding one of those mechanical bulls.

Then I pictured my return home. Just inside the door, I'd drop my parcels, and tear into them. I'd show my wife the fine things I'd found on my trip to Rochester. I pictured her expression of delight, and pride in the shrewd purchases I'd made—and then I saw her rolling on the floor, convulsed with laughter, speechless, pointing at me in my lime-green Roy Rogers suit.

"Naw, Bill. I think I'll pass 'em up."

The cowboy suits I'd wanted since the age of six remain up there in Rochester, hanging under the rafters like multi-colored bats. Riding home on the train I realized that once again I'd chickened out. I tore into a cellophane-wrapped doughnut, and listened to that lonesome whistle blow.

❧ ❧ ❧

My father gave out few details about his early life. I knew he had come from Poland. He had managed to avoid military service in the First World War, and shortly after had walked across Germany and France on his way to America.

Apparently, there were shipboard operators who'd rent you a bankroll to show the immigration officials, proving you had means of support—and you'd hand over the money when you landed.

My father arrived in New York with a little more than two dollars in his pocket. He slept in parked cars for a while. He got work as a waiter at resorts in the Catskill Mountains, sold things from a pushcart on the Lower East Side, did a little bootlegging, migrated west to Chicago, south to Texas, and then to Tennessee.

Occasionally, he would say cryptic things.

"Sonnye, vhen I vas a boy in Poland, I used to fly like a pigeon," he would say. This was entirely cryptic.

Other things he said were partially cryptic. "Sonnye, vhen I vas a boy in Poland, of mine seven brudders, I vas deh only vun who didn' hev to carry ah pistol."

"Your brothers all carried pistols?"

"Yeh, but I didn' hev to hev vun because I vas so tough."

"Why did your brothers carry pistols?"

"Hah? Did you did your homevork? Go already! Study!"

5

These fragments—and there are few of them—I was able to piece together to form a picture of the character my father might have been in the old country. And that character I later found in literature. It was Benya Krik, a character in stories by Isaac Babel—a real good writer.

Benya Krik is a sort of Ukrainian Mack the Knife—a dandy in cream-colored trousers and raspberry-red shoes—a gentleman gangster, given to writing polite letters to his unwilling business associates. For example:

Mr. Eichbaum,
Please have the kindness to slip twenty thousand rubles under the gate at 17 Sophia Street tomorrow morning. If you don't do this, you can expect something unheard of, something that all Odessa will talk about. Yours respectfully,

Benya the King

How similar Benya the King's character and enterprises were to my father's I learned when a seldom-seen cousin named Frederick, who had known my father in Warsaw, told me stories of his doings there.

I don't want anyone to get the idea that my father was vicious or crooked, just because he was apparently a holdup man in his early life. It was a little different back there and back then.

Opportunities were limited in the ghetto, Cousin Frederick explained. Certain able-bodied young Jews, rather than suffer poverty and inactivity, went into the business of hijacking things from other Jews.

Goods were taken from place to place by horse-drawn wagon and, later, trucks. The driver would be distracted, one way or another, and some of these goods would come into the hands of my father, and his colleagues and brothers. The purpose was not to keep these goods, or to sell them for profit—but to return them to their rightful owner.

Naturally, a suitable reward was expected.

A letter such as Benya's would be sent to the consignee; compensation would be negotiated. Commerce flourished. Life went on. Cases of shooting and arson were infrequent.

Now, my father's involvement in this sort of enterprise is entirely surmise, based on Cousin Frederick's stories, the odd remark my father had made about packing a rod, and the like.

My father, by the time I knew him, was the soul of rectitude. Still, his style of attire, the way he carried himself, his penchant for shiny automobiles, and his simple, yet frightening, manner of expression were all consistent with the Odessa mobsters as Isaac Babel depicted them.

But I never knew him to push anybody around. Except me. My brothers. My mother. And his business associates.

※ ※ ※

M Y father used to tell me about an incident that took place during his first few days in America. He was starving, living on the streets of New York, sleeping in parked cars.

He had nothing in his pocket, and nothing in his belly.

He couldn't bring himself to beg.

According to some family stories, he'd been a holdup man in the old country, but on this side of the water, he was Lincolnesque in his honesty, and was known to come back years later to repay a quarter or a dime.

But this time he was perishing. He had to do something. There was a restaurant on Second Avenue called Thau's. A bowl of soup cost a nickel, and there was a basket of rolls on every table. My father went in and ordered soup, knowing he would not be able to pay for it.

While he was eating his soup, and wolfing rolls, another patron was staring at him. My father stared back. The guy looked vaguely familiar.

"Don' I know you frum Varsaw?" the stranger asked.

"Yeh. Maybe. You look familiar," my father answered.

The stranger joined him. They fell to talking about people they knew, and places they'd been.

My father conceived a desperate idea. He ordered a sandwich. A cup of coffee. It would be the police, prison, and God knew what if his companion failed to pick up the tab.

But he did. He paid for the meal, they shook hands, and went their separate ways.

Forty years later, I was going to school in upstate New York, and my father had come to the city on business. I met him for lunch at Thau's.

The place hadn't changed at all. The coats of paint on the pressed-tin ceiling and the coat hooks were so numerous that the interior had a quasi-organic appearance. The tables and chairs looked as if they'd grown there too.

There were the baskets of rolls on the tables. I had soup.

My father spoke to the waiter. "See dat guy over dere? Don' say nawthin' to 'im, but put his lonch on my teb."

🐾 🐾 🐾

My father was an expert in dealing with banks. Throughout his business career he was always able to borrow comparatively huge sums with no collateral.

His first experience with borrowing set the tone for the rest of his life. He'd seen a way to make some money on a carload of surplus shoes, and he bid on it. When his bid was accepted, he needed money to cover it. My mother told him to get a haircut and put on his suit, go to the bank, and ask for a loan.

What he did was go to the bank in his overalls. "I don't own nothing but mine brains," he told the bank president—in those days when you wanted to borrow money, you talked to the president—"but I never didn't paid back money vhat I owed." He got the loan. Then he had a haircut and put on his suit and came back to tell my mother.

In later years, he would appear at the Amalgamated National Bank in Chicago every Christmastime with an armload of kosher salamis. The salamis would be wrapped in Christmas paper and of varying sizes. Each teller would receive a one-foot salami. Senior tellers got two-footers. Vice presidents received yard-long salamis, and the president got a salami five feet long. The people at the bank loved him.

He continued to own nothing, made perilous deals, borrowed large sums frequently, and never failed to repay on time.

They don't make guys like my father anymore. And it's impossible to find those five-foot salamis, too.

꽃 꽃 꽃

I'M told that as a toddler of less than two I appeared one day in our living room in Memphis, Tennessee, holding by the tails a brace of dead Norway rats, one in each hand. I must have taken them out of traps in the kitchen. We had plenty of rats, and not a great deal else.

The period during which we lived in Memphis was marked by the winding down of the Great Depression and the beginning of the Second World War. It was at this time that my father first began to have some success in business.

Some time before war broke out, he had borrowed money to buy a carload of worn-out army boots. He had figured a way to refurbish them assembly-line style, and had set up a little shop to do so. The idea was to sell them as work boots. War came, and my father wound up selling the boots back to the army. He then patriotically offered to teach them his method of restoring the boots, effectively putting himself out of business, but winning the gratitude of some majors in charge of purchasing.

The boot transaction left him with capital for the first time in his life, and his connections with the supply officers made further deals possible. My father had been in this country for twenty years, angling for some kind of a chance. Now that he had it, he developed it energetically. He traveled all over the country buying up and selling lots of this and that.

We left Memphis, Tennessee, and moved to Chicago, to a big apartment, without rats, a half-block from Lake Shore Drive.

It was while living in that apartment I first entered that part of my life I consciously recollect. I went from crawling to walking to playing outdoors and going to school while we lived there—about six years.

I've often wondered who and what I might have become had I grown up living there, had I gone through elementary school and high school living in one place, knowing the same people, the same streets.

But it wasn't like that for me, or the rest of my family. My father liked to move about. By the time I was ready for college, we had changed domiciles thirteen times, swapped cities six times, and I had attended ten schools.

Through all of this—which is to say through my entire life—I regarded Chicago, and that first large apartment, as home. I used to dream of living there, and frequently imagine it as the setting for works of fiction I write. But, having left Chicago at the age of seven or eight, I didn't get back until I was about fourteen years of age, the summer before I was to begin high school.

In my family—and in the nation in general, to a greater extent than today—high school was regarded as the jumping-off place for genuine endeavors. People went to work, went to war, and got married right out of high school—some without graduating. So if one was a high-school student, one was regarded as grown-up, and free to come and go, keep what hours one wanted, and with a minimum of questions or supervision. So, all of a sudden, I had freedom of movement.

What was more, our last stop, for a number of years, had been Los Angeles, California, famous for its relative featurelessness, its dearth of public transport and prohibitive pedestrian distances between points. In Chicago I was not only free to go wherever I wanted, but had places to go and ways to get there.

I began my practice of urban tourism, which continues to this day. I wandered everywhere, walking for hours—took buses to the end of the line, just to see where they would go—prowled around strange neighborhoods—and studied maps of the city.

My object was to find the old, the ornate, the quaint, and the bizarre. I was developing an eye for architecture and statuary, though I didn't know it.

I found Bohemian beer gardens, in which I would be served without question; old enclaves of Bohemians of another sort—whole blocks in which the houses had been designed and decorated according to some aesthetic movement now more or less forgotten; little villages within the city, farmhouses interspersed between apartment towers; little ethnic communities existing almost autonomously within the greater city, with nobody speaking English. I found secondhand bookshops, some vast and inexhaustible, some tiny, hidden away on neighborhood streets. I ventured into the suburban fringe, and found great postwar expanses of nothing in particular. And I explored the buildings in the Loop, some of them treasure-houses, like the Fine Arts Building, and Roosevelt University, formerly the Louis Sullivan opera house.

I tramped and rode buses alone, observing silently, storing up impressions. What I was doing, it turned out, was preparing for the trade I would follow later, and did not dream of then.

I suppose that's why I'm patient with aimless louts to this day—bumming and gestating look a lot alike.

※ ※ ※

DURING World War Two, ensconced in the big apartment, and with money coming in, my father indulged heavily in the honorable tradition of "bringing people home." He expanded this from the Jewish practice of inviting a poor or friendless stranger to the Sabbath meal to taking people in to live with us for long periods.

Most unusual was a contingent of rabbis recently arrived from Shanghai. I remember them carrying chairs from the dining room in to the living room, and sitting in a circle, drinking whiskey out of little glasses and engaging in a heated conversation with my father, who appeared to be delighted.

For a long time the Polish Anthropologist and her husband the Political Activist lived in the back bedroom. Sonia, the Anthropologist, was working on a secret project for the War Department. She was studying Japanese culture with an eye toward developing more effective propaganda—and by way of contributing something as rent, and keeping in the mood, did most of the cooking for the family. It was a kind of Nippo-Polish cuisine.

Her husband spent his days at the dining room table, pounding out scripts for speeches that he would deliver at nightly meetings of obscure groups and committees out to win the war by talking.

But my absolute favorite resident of the back bedroom was Uncle Boris. He was not a refugee as such. Uncle Boris was my father's brother, a professional houseguest. A forger of documents in the old country, Uncle Boris was apt to engage in shady enterprises at which he tended to get caught. On more than one occasion he had backed a truck up to my father's store at night and removed the goods. My father liked having Uncle Boris live with us. He could keep an eye on him, and it was cheaper to house and feed him directly.

Barred from exercising any of his professions while living with us, Boris was free to give all his time to Art and tinkering. Cinema was his artform of choice, and I would go with him to the park daily, where, with my father's movie camera, we would shoot hundreds of feet of squirrels at play.

I myself appeared as an actor in the film that resulted from these excursions, "Sonny-Boy in the Park with Squirrels." All of my scenes featured me, offering tidbits to semitame rodents, and the edited work ran feature-length, like all of Boris's movies.

Boris and I also flew kites, and paid many visits to the zoo, where we planned to make another major project, "Sonny-Boy at the Zoo." More ambitious than "Squirrels," this film was to pair me with Bushman, the Lincoln Park Zoo's well-beloved gorilla, a particular favorite of mine. It often happens that short-sighted businessmen squelch the plans of creative directors, and in this case it was my father who cut off Boris's credit at the photo-finishers.

When he had funds, Boris would reside in fashionable resort hotels. There he would economize on meals by living off a salami, which, along with a poundcake and a sharp knife, he would keep in a bureau drawer. He looked like Erich von Stroheim, and had a number of nifty outfits, complete with hand-painted neckties. His object, while residing at these hotels, was to find a suitable widow. He found one, Zelda, and married her, only to discover afterward that she, too, kept a salami and a poundcake in her room. They continued visiting friends and relatives, his and hers, for a number of years. I think they viewed themselves as a sort of Yiddish version of the Duke and Duchess of Windsor.

In time, Boris and Zelda migrated to Brooklyn, where Boris found congenial work altering the provenance of antique artifacts. Periodically, some member of the family would receive a garish tureen or a set of quasi-Dresden figurines, or, in the case of one of my sisters, an enormous ormolu lobster—a centerpiece of some sort. Having received one of these objets d'art, one would dispatch a note of thanks to Boris, who would counter with a letter saying, "I knew you were looking for a piece like that, so I bought it for you at a good price." And he'd enclose a bill.

Boris was an important early influence. He taught me the value of leisure for a creative man, and the many points of connection between Art and Crime.

※ ※ ※

I GRANT that I did not watch television from my bassinet, as subsequent generations of vidiots have done. And I did have a couple of years of exposure to pre-TV culture. When I got to college it was still an expulsion offense to smuggle a set into the dorm—but such instances of video deprivation, which I sometimes weave into tales to astonish the young, do not signify. For better or worse, I grew up with the tube, like most people now alive.

It was in 1948 that television took over. At the beginning of that year there were 19 TV stations in operation and about 175,000 sets in American homes. At year's end there were 47 stations broadcasting and a million sets in place.

After that it was just a matter of numbers—what television would become and what it would make of us was manifested and even refined in that first year.

I was in on it. My older brother, with the first paycheck from his first job, surprised the family by bringing home an RCA—I think it had a nine-inch screen, a super luxury model. It was set up in the living room, and a row of straight chairs was placed in front of it.

I remember the first televised image we saw on that first night. It was a bunch of mountaineers, with forked beards, sitting in a row, on chairs, playing jugs and spoons and stamping their bare feet.

I remember thinking that the hillbillies resembled the antique photos of some of the ancestors my father had left Europe to get away from. He resented having been born on the other side, and in the nineteenth century, which he regarded as benighted and backward.

"I yam no beck nomberr," he would say. "I yam a tventiet' century man."

He had been profoundly impressed by the New York World's Fair in 1939, and considered it his duty as an American to buy into the world of the future. As new inventions and gimmicks were created, he got hold of them. The war had cut off the availability of modernist household gadgets, but now the flow was steady, and we had the electric juicer, home movies, and a vacuum cleaner that resembled the family Buick.

My brother had beaten my father to the punch badly by bringing home the TV set, and perhaps even "gone too far," and shown disrespect. But my father did not decry the undertaking as a waste of time, nor suggest that my brother had fallen for hype advertising by purchasing an inferior black-and-white set, when surely, Technicolor was not more than a few months away. He knew or sensed that anything of that sort would be sacrilege. He took his place in the row of chairs in the darkness, and marveled at the hillbilly band. Talking pictures piped right into the living room, he suddenly realized, was what America was all about. And of course, everybody else was realizing the same thing in 1948.

While the rest of the family was still getting used to having a television, one of us was ready to begin to worship the box with his whole heart and live his life by the flickering blue light. That was me. I discovered the afternoon children's programs—western movies, ancient cartoons, and puppet shows. By the simple expedient of eliminating healthy outdoor exercise, the likes of myself had time to view them in the hours between the end of school and suppertime. I was the first to be sacrificed (willingly, mind you) on the electronic altar.

My father was to establish a relationship with the set as intimate as my own. A year or so after the family's first exposure, he acquired a much larger set, and rearranged a spare bedroom into what would later be called "the den." He shifted an old couch into the room, and easy chairs, discovered the newly invented trays with folding legs of tubular metal, and assumed his rightful place as impresario of our little home theater. He would dust the cabinet of the television, and polish the screen. During commercials he would disappear into the kitchen and bring us ice cream, scooped by his own hand. (About this time, my brother moved into his own apartment, taking the little RCA with him, and began to see a psychoanalyst.)

My father took to viewing wrestling with enthusiasm, was a shrewd and critical watcher of the news, and enjoyed an occasional drama, if it was live. He refused to look at reruns, even if he hadn't seen the show the first time.

"I didn' paid out four hunnerd dollars for this fine television to look on old programs," he'd say. Somehow I think he'd have approved of MTV.

❊ ❊ ❊

MY earliest memories of going to school in Chicago are something like the film about Scott of the Antarctic that was on TV the other night. I had to cover about five blocks to the Louis B. Nettlehorst Elementary School, and in winter it was a test of strength, native cunning, dead reckoning, and the will to survive.

The cold-weather gear in use in those days was the dreaded snowsuit. One was variously buttoned, zippered, strapped, and buckled into it. I believe it was an adaptation of the standard closed-type diving suit without the brass headpiece with the windows, in place of which there was a leather aviator's helmet that buckled under the chin and was reinforced by three or four turns of a woolen muffler.

There was no way to put the arms down against the sides, knee movement was limited, and should a kid fall down, he'd remain there immobile until someone set him on his feet again.

Kids who wore glasses, as I did, were further impaired as wisps of breath coming up from under the muffler would cause the lenses to fog. The danger was overshooting the school, and waddling off into terra incognita. One had to depend a lot on smells and sounds to get safely to the classroom.

I still wake up screaming when I dream of unsuiting in

the dim and crowded cloakroom. It must have looked like twenty-five or thirty tiny Houdinis doing the straitjacket trick among the lumps of melting snow. And six or so hours later, we'd have to get back into the life-support outfits for the voyage home.

I won't dwell on the evils of the diabolical five-buckle galoshes except to say that no one in history has ever succeeded in fastening them.

So you can imagine with what gratitude spring was welcomed at the Louis B. Nettlehorst School. We would congregate before school in the playground, which was surfaced with a special sharp-edged gravel that, when one made sudden contact with it, would invariably result in honorable wounds.

Scooping away the gravel, we would expose the permafrost and create surfaces for the marble and top seasons. These came in their turn each spring. It would be marbles for a while—and then, one day, tops. Followed a few weeks later by yo-yos. The yo-yo season was the apex of the social year. Something like boat races on the Thames at Oxford.

The event that gave yo-yo-ing such class was the appearance of Manuel, a Filipino guy in a gold sport jacket. He was a yo-yo virtuoso. He was just there, in the schoolyard one day, doing amazing tricks with two yo-yos, then with four! It was astonishing. And he gave away little booklets—for free! They were put out by the Duncan Yo-Yo Company, and they contained instructions for doing all the tricks the guy in the cloth-of-gold jacket had done.

Of course, you had to have an official Tournament Duncan Yo-Yo to get really good results. The idea was that Manuel was going to come back. He'd hold a yo-yo tourney right in our schoolyard, and the winners would receive special golden Duncan Yo-Yos with five rhinestones on each side. These yo-yos could not be bought in any store.

I invested in a suitable yo-yo. Deep cherry red it was, with a shpritz of black paint across each side. Beautiful, and stamped in gold with the words *Official, Tournament, Duncan*. And I practiced. I learned the basic maneuver— the sleeper. Then walk the dog. Rock the baby. Around the world. The wrist flip. The double wrist flip. I achieved technical mastery. I began to develop a style. I created a wicked variation of the double wrist flip, which I combined with a half-arc. I was good. I knew it. The golden rhinestone yo-yo would be mine.

Except the guy in the sport jacket never came back. Summer passed. Autumn flashed by. The desolate winter returned. Snowsuits. Five-buckle galoshes. Darkness and biting wind. Spring. Marbles. Tops. Then—scores of kids with newly strung Official Duncan Tournament Yo-Yos and foxed and dog-eared yo-yo manuals. But no Manuel.

The next year he did not come. Nor the next. I kept in practice. I stayed ready. I still had that yo-yo book with me when I went to college. I guess I was twenty-two when I realized that Manuel was never going to turn up—and that this is a false world.

※ ※ ※

When it was time for me to begin high school, my family moved from Los Angeles to Chicago. We moved into a brand-new apartment house, and I was sent to a school where I didn't know anybody.

One day, my mother said to me, "Do you know Mrs. Prince's boy, Bill?"

I said I hadn't met any Bill Prince.

"He's a very nice boy," my mother said. "Serious. He's coming to see you this afternoon."

"Aww, Mother! You know I hate this sort of thing."

"Hate what? What do you hate? What is there to hate? A very nice boy—and he's a senior—wants to take time to get acquainted with you (who have nothing to offer). You should be grateful."

A little while later a boy who could only be described as beautiful arrived. He had wavy blond hair and skin like porcelain. My mother introduced us and brought us Cokes. We were to have our visit in my room.

When we were alone, Bill Prince said, "I am a homosexual."

He was the first identified homosexual I ever met. I resolved to be cool. So I didn't say, "Really?" or anything stupid like that. Instead I said, "It would be a shame if you were anything else."

"That's how I feel about it," Bill Prince said. "So it doesn't give you a problem?"

"Why should it give me a problem?" I asked, thinking, "I will be careful never to be seen with this guy."

"Good," Bill Prince said. "What I came to see you about was my political campaign."

"Your political campaign?"

"I'm running for student body president. Will you support me?"

This was the mid-fifties, in a particularly unenlightened high school. Any minute shade of difference meant ostracism.

"You're nuts," I told him.

"Why do you say that?" Bill Prince asked.

"I mean . . . do you tell everybody that you're . . . um . . . ah . . . ?"

"That I'm gay? Sure."

"Well, nobody's going to vote for you," I said.

"Would you vote for me?"

"Yeh, well . . . I guess I . . . yes . . . sure. I'll vote for you."

"See? It's no problem. I've got charisma. When people meet me, they like me."

"I wouldn't go so far as to say I like you."

"But you agreed to vote for me. That's the important thing. Now ... will you agree to be on my campaign staff?"

Humor him, I figured. "What do I have to do?"

"Jim Mooney is my campaign manager. He'll get in touch with you."

Nobody ever got in touch with me. The next time I saw Bill Prince he was on the stage of the auditorium with the other candidates for student body president. He made a terrible speech.

He got almost no votes. Somebody on the football team got elected.

The next day, I met Jim Mooney. He had incredibly thick glasses, and I identified him as a member of the sight-saving class. The nearly blind students always hung out together. It turned out they were the political machine in the school.

Jim Mooney handed me a rectangle of felt, an armband, with the words HALL GUARD LT. sewn onto it.

"Our candidate lost, but your work is appreciated," Jim Mooney told me. He also told me that I was now a lieutenant in the hall guards, and had the right to wander the halls at will without an official pass. One period a day, instead of going to study hall, I was to patrol the entire building, and make sure that the hall guards—kids whose duty it was to ask ordinary citizens to show their passes—were at their posts. I was also free to step outside and have a smoke, or an extra lunch, if so inclined.

The following semester I was also commissioned lieutenant fire marshal, which meant I was to know the location of all fire extinguishers and was informed of fire drills before they took place. And as people graduated, I ultimately inherited the positions of captain of hall guards and chief fire marshal, which empowered me to leave any class without excuse or prior warning, and to be anywhere in the school at any time. I even had a set of keys.

Bill Prince learned to stop mentioning his sexual orientation, was elected to the state legislature, and is prominent in Illinois politics. Jim Mooney took holy orders and made a brilliant career in the Society of Jesus. And I, once and forever, learned the importance of voting in local elections.

※ ※ ※

As a high-school kid in Chicago, very often, after school, or instead of going to school, I'd catch the number 151 bus and head for the Loop. The Loop is the downtown, the business district, where the tall buildings are.

I'd always hit the main library, splendid within with white marble and gaudy mosaics. There, I'd spend some time reading. My favorite spot there was the music manuscript room, which was never crowded.

I had a favorite coffee shop as well, chosen for the best deal in the house, the chopped ham salad sandwich—which tasted ghastly, but cost only a quarter.

The point of saving money on food was in order to have it to spend on tobacco. The Palmer House hotel had a sort of gallery above the main lobby where a boy might sit in a comfortable armchair, doing his homework and observing the passing scene while enjoying a Havana cigar.

When night came, and the commuters were beginning to shift for home, it would be time to visit the Department of Water and Sewers in City Hall.

This was where my friend Harry Saphire worked evenings. His father, an employee of the department, was dead. In the good old Chicago tradition, the son of the loyal city employee and party regular was given his father's salary so the bereaved family would not be without. The son, a full-time high-school student, was not expected to take over his father's actual duties—he was just to show up every night, and sit in the Department of Water and Sewers, doing his homework. Come election time, he'd help get out the vote. Patronage at its best and most humane.

Harry would be alone in the vast Department of Water and Sewers. One figure, at one of the hundred desks, all the lights burning in order for him to read his history assignment. He'd be glad of some company, and get me a cup of free municipal coffee. We'd sit around the department, talking—and sometimes go down the wide staircase in the middle of the department to the glorious thing that was housed beneath.

It was the traffic-light control board for the City of Chicago. A darkened room with a vast map taking up one wall. Every traffic light was represented by a tiny set of lights on the map, blinking, going from green to yellow to red and then to green. It was as fine as anything in any museum.

And before the wall was the control panel—hundreds of switches, and two great knobs. It was easily figured out, and the person in control of that panel controlled the flow of traffic, throughout the great city. It was possible to cause a single light, at a given intersection, to remain red for five minutes, then green for thirty seconds, then red for ten minutes.

The Loop would be virtually empty by now—the bulk of traffic approaching the suburbs—so we would hear no horns, or shouts, or screeching of brakes, as with the mighty knobs we caused traffic throughout the city to progress in a manner too sprightly for comfort—or hellishly slow.

I like to think we didn't kill anyone. I can't say that it

crossed our minds at the time. We always timed the green lights to give a *Chicago* pedestrian a reasonable chance. Out-of-towners have always been on their own.

᠉ ᠉ ᠉

W HEN I was eleven or twelve, living in Los Angeles, I took to walking long distances on Saturdays. My destination was usually something called the Town and Country Market, an early precursor of the shopping mall, some two hours on foot from my house.

When I got there, I'd hang around for a while, looking in the various shops, maybe buying a comic book or a hamburger, and then trudge home. One of the stores that fascinated me was a place that sold art supplies. It had the sort of appeal for me that a shop which sold model airplanes might have had. I liked the displays of brushes and tools, and colors.

In a glass case was a drawing outfit that included a selection of Hunt's Crow Quill pens, a pen holder, a bottle of India ink, little sheets of drawing paper, and a booklet that told how to do it. Price, three-fifty.

It appealed to me. I considered it for a couple of weeks, while saving up money—and finally bought it and carried it home.

My experience with model airplane kits and educational toys had fully prepared me to deal with my drawing kit. As I never do anymore, I read the instructions before fooling with any of the components. The booklet was simple and concise. It showed various examples of drawings made with Hunt's Crow Quill pens, and told you how to dip the things in the ink and skritch on the paper with them. There were examples of various kinds of shading and cross-hatching.

One of the examples in the booklet was a winter land-scape with leafless trees. I decided to try something like that. Now I am remembering the first time I ever made a mark with India ink, blacker than anything I'd ever seen, on that creamy, thick paper. It was wonderful!

I drew a whole tree, gnarled and naked, the boughs, branches, and twigs stark and dramatic against the white. The trunk, shaded. It had a lonesome, agonized appearance. I thought it was beautiful. I handled the bottom, where the roots spread out against the ground, pretty well too, I thought.

I did a whole bunch of trees. They got better and better. I experienced for the first time what an artist experiences. Then the other thing that artists experience happened. I wanted to show them to someone.

I had an aunt by marriage, Marilyn. She was the youngest adult in the family, and I admired her. Marilyn was an artist. She took classes at night. She had copied a record album cover, and framed the result—a portrait of Johnny Mathis. It hung in her living room. She had also done an oil painting of a vase of flowers. A still-life. She was too good for our family, and said so. Later, she left my uncle, who took it very well.

I showed my drawings to Aunt Marilyn, who happened to be hanging around the house.

"You never drew these," she said.

She took the drawings into the living room, where my father and mother were watching television.

"Your son is a liar," she said. "He showed me these drawings, which were obviously done by some older boy, and is passing them off as his own."

"I did too draw those," I said.

"Don't make it worse," Aunt Marilyn said to me. "He couldn't possibly have drawn them," she said to my parents. "I am an artist. I know about these things."

"I drew them. I could do it again."

"He's going to be a criminal," Aunt Marilyn said. "You're his parents. What are you going to do about it?"

"Don't tell lies and upset your aunt," my father said.

I ran across one of those drawings, used as a bookmark, not long ago. I still like it.

Doubtless, my father was just trying to shut Marilyn up so he and my mother could go back to watching Abbott and Costello. Doubtless, he forgot the whole incident in the next minute. But I would remember it.

I could have argued more, but I was too stung by what Marilyn had said, and the realization that it would be a mistake to ever again let these people, these adults I lived with, know what I was doing. I never tried to draw again while I lived at home. The India ink dried in the bottle, and the Hunt's Crow Quill pens rusted.

But my adventures in art were not over—only postponed.

🎋 🎋 🎋

ONCE my father visited me at college. I heard a knock at my door, and there he was.

"So, sonnye. You're surprised to see me, ha?"

Surprised and terrified. My father was not given to visiting, and when he did, it could only be to bring bad news. He had never dropped in on me before, but there were plenty of family stories—all of them disquieting. Since he had gone a thousand miles out of his way, I had reason to believe this would be something horrific.

"I'm t'inking of pulling you oudt frum dis collitch."

That was horrific enough for me. I liked being in college. For one thing it meant I was not at home, working for him. My brothers worked for him. They had nervous tics, and were given to staring into space with doomed expressions.

Going to work for my father was something like being in the French Foreign Legion or the Turkish navy, only not as much fun. I'd had five or six summers of it, and was ready to do anything to avoid it happening again.

"Why take me out of college? I'm doing good."

"You're doing lousy. Alrady you majored in English, philosophy, history, and drama. Every semester you svitch. You'll be here ten years before you'll finish."

That was my plan exactly. I was currently majoring in religion, and thinking about switching to economics.

"So, I'm t'inking after dis semester you'll come home. I hev somptin' you can do."

My father's business enterprises changed from time to time, but they always included a dirty, rat-infested basement, where one could sort rags, or scrape crud off war-surplus binnacles, or stack heavy filthy objects on top of one another.

"Look, what do I have to do to stay in school?" I knew I had a chance. He was never tentative. If he'd made up his mind, he would have just told me to start packing.

"I'll let you stay, if you pick sompin' and do it vit all your might for deh nex' two years."

"Pick something?"

"Pick anyt'ing."

"Anything?"

"Anyt'ing, but remember, vhatever you'll pick, you'll got to do it for two years. Steady."

"How about if I pick art?"

"Vhatever. Just you'll do nawthin' else until you graduate outta here."

I didn't know why I said art. Until that moment, I hadn't considered it seriously. I was taking a studio course in sculpture, but that was only because there was no reading required. I was getting an A, but so did everyone who successfully created a clay model of their own head, using mirrors and calipers.

If a kid was talented, and could slap a likeness together in a couple of weeks, it made no difference. Charles Boggs, the sculpture professor, would keep us working on the things until the end of the semester. The heads all wound up smooth and spooky with sightless eyeballs. After we had smoothed and smoothed our clay clones, we were taught to make molds, and cast them in plaster. As horrible as they had looked in clay, when they were stark chalky white they became truly ghastly. Nobody took their heads home. Instead, deathly faces of students present and past lined the shelves around the top of the studio.

Few people signed up for a second semester of sculpture, which was how Professor Boggs liked it. He had gotten off by heart the routine of teaching heads. He could have done it in his sleep. I can hear him today:

"The eye is like a marble. The teeth are like a horseshoe. Take the calipers and measure from the crown of the head to the point of the chin. The next measurement is taken across the head, from cheekbone to cheekbone." He could have been dead and still given his spiel. Some said he was.

It was also said that Boggs never switched off the engine in his Volkswagen when he came to teach. He may not have been much of a sculptor, but he was a real professional when it came to the fine points of being a college teacher.

But I had made my deal with my father. I was going to specialize in art—and the only art I had done so far was Sculpture 101. I went to Professor Boggs, and told him I had decided to major in art.

"Really?" Boggs said sucking at his pipe. "You'll never make any money at it, you know . . . unless you teach. If you're going to study art, you may as well start getting some experience teaching right away. Now here's what I propose. You will teach all three sections of Sculpture 101."

"Me?"

"Just remember, the eye is like a marble, the teeth are like a horseshoe, the tops of the ears are even with the level of the eye. It's quite simple. If you run into any problems see me. I'll be here on Wednesdays."

"I'm not sure I can do this."

"The only way to get experience is to wade right in. I'll also make you studio monitor. You'll keep the place clean, help the other students cast their heads, keep the clay wet. I'll pay you fifty dollars a semester."

"I'm not sure . . . I . . ."

"I'll give you my home phone number. If anyone comes looking for me from the office, tell them I stepped out for a minute, and ring me up."

"I . . . uh . . ."

"Here's the key to my office. You may look at my nudist magazines. Pick a subject for a figure study. We'll talk about it later. And, Pinkwater . . . better not to mention our arrangement to anyone on the faculty. They're not very progressive." I hardly ever saw him again.

Thus began my formal education as an artist. To this day, there are graduates of St. Leon's College who believe that I, Charles Boggs, was the one who taught them that the eye is like a marble.

※ ※ ※

I USED to be a jerk, a wimp, and a weenie. I was a sissy. And a big fat sissy to boot. I was so shy and uncomfortable that my very presence inflicted agony on everyone I met, adults especially.

I was such a specimen well into my time at college when I decided to major in art. The Art Department at St. Leon's College was lousy. Three professors, two much worse than average, and one merely worse. Worst of all was Charles

Boggs, the sculpture teacher, who exploited and despised me.

But I liked the place. I had made friends there, and couldn't bear the idea of having to reestablish myself somewhere else. So when I decided to transfer to the Art Department, I did not do the reasonable thing and also transfer to another school, but persuaded myself that I could learn what I needed.

Of course, right away I began to suffer from instructional malnutrition. If I was going to learn anything about art, I was going to have to improvise.

At this particular college, they would turn us loose for better than two months in the wintertime. During this period we were supposed to find a job relating to our field of study, do a research project, write something, or otherwise profitably employ the time.

I got a job as an intern in a sculpture foundry. I was such a wuss that I had *my mother* phone the place up and make the arrangements. They never saw or heard me until I showed up for work.

I was to have a corner in which to sculpt, the guy who ran the place would give me a few pointers, and I would help out with what went on there. Exactly what that was, I found out at the same time I discovered I had a fear of molten metal.

This was a place where sculptors would bring their work in clay or plaster. A mold would be made and then a wax cast, which would then be surrounded with a fireproof plaster form, the wax melted out in huge ovens, and molten bronze poured into the space where the wax image had been.

I had read the *Autobiography* of Benvenuto Cellini. I knew about the romance of bronze casting. However, when the actual stuff was hot enough to vaporize flesh, I'd find reasons to be someplace else. The rest of the time, I swept, scraped crud off fire bricks, crawled around inside the ovens used for melting wax out of molds—and most of all, avoided Nunzio DiNapoli, the proprietor.

Now, Nunzio was a guy whose background, experience, manner, and outlook all related to the steel mills south of Chicago, where he'd grown up. He was a good sculptor, and probably a nice guy, but he was not able to deal with a nineteen-year-old, 240-pound, prissy pseudointellectual. Nunzio wore steel-soled foundry shoes, a bandana around his neck, spat tobacco juice through his teeth, and had to shave all the way down to his collarbone—twice a day. I was so scared of Nunzio that whenever he talked to me, I'd become inarticulate, and behave like a simpering oaf.

Nunzio, for his part, appeared to be very uncomfortable around me, possibly because the piece of sculpture on which I was working, and which he was supposed to criticize, was so horrible that the only response a decent human being could have had would have been to smash it to bits and then kill me.

"Uhhhn. It's comin' along very nice, kid," Nunzio Di-Napoli would say, and make tracks for somewhere else.

I contrived to avoid these moments by coming in before dawn. I'd do my various chores, run out of the building as soon as Nunzio arrived, hide out at the zoo, or the Clark Theater if I had the price, and come back at night when he was gone.

Upstairs above the bronze foundry were some studios, cubicles that were rented out to artists. Only one of them was occupied around the clock. This older guy—must have been about forty—appeared to have worked out a deal whereby he'd serve as a sort of night watchman in exchange for his rent.

Navin Diebold he was called. He was a sculptor, but not the earthy kind like DiNapoli. He'd come downstairs sometimes, when I was working on my horrible figurine late at night, and smoke a cigarette and chat for a while.

I wasn't afraid of Diebold. Even though he seemed to study me—look at me with one eye—I felt comfortable with him, maybe because he seemed highly nervous and jumpy himself. He stayed off the subject of sculpture, and I did too.

I was grateful to Diebold for that. It had begun to dawn on me that it was a sin for someone like me to attempt to make sculpture. I had plans to take a stab at painting and printmaking when I got back to college—but the indications were that it would be a fatal stab—more of a slash. And yet I was stuck with it. I had more than a year to go in my pact with my father. It was do art or work for him, testing and repairing defective air mattresses.

For his part, my father was enjoying the whole business.

"Vell, Mister Artist, how's by you deh voild of aesthetics?"

"Lousy, Dad. Lousy."

🌿 🌿 🌿

DURING my spring semester as an art major at St. Leon's College, Charles Boggs, the sculpture professor, permitted me to drop teaching two of the three sections of Sculpture 101, when I begged him on the grounds that I was failing all my other classes. He did cut my pay as studio monitor to twenty-five dollars per semester, but to show that he wasn't mad at me, he told me that he was going to allow me to begin carving in wood. He sold me a hunk of oak from his own garage for fifty dollars, and told me to carve a figure.

The piece of oak was long and narrow, so I began cultivating girls of that general shape, hoping to persuade one of them to pose for me. At that time, short, vivacious, and pneumatic were the preferred physical traits for women, and beanpole types had time on their hands. I got to see a number of them naked, which gave me status among my friends.

I whittled on that log for months. As I worked, it took on various shapes. Most of the time it resembled a knobkerrie or a Fijian war club. Never a human woman, or anything inspired by one. My models left me, disgusted or insulted.

The painting teacher, Shandar Papescu, was a personal friend of Professor Boggs. He set up a bunch of dried pussy willows in an old coal-oil can, along with some other oddments of trash, and had us draw that with charcoal for sixteen weeks. The advanced class was allowed to paint the arrangement in oil.

I was learning nothing! I needed someone to set me straight.

School ended for the summer. I found myself back in Chicago. I was desperate to get some advice. There were two artists known to me. One was Nunzio DiNapoli, of whom I was afraid. The other was that curious guy, Navin Diebold, who had been the night-watchman in the bronze foundry where I'd worked the previous winter. I went to see him.

"I was wondering if you gave lessons."

"That depends."

"I've got about thirty dollars. Would you be willing to teach me something about art for that?"

"What did you have in mind?"

"Well, anything would help. I sort of don't know what I'm doing."

"I'll have to think it over. Do you have any work that I could see?"

"I've got a figure I carved. I could show you that."

"Bring it around at four o'clock on Tuesday."

The following Tuesday, I hoisted my sculpture onto my back and brought it to Diebold's studio. He looked at it for a long time.

"This is a piece of crap," he said. Then there was a very long pause. "But I'm sufficiently impressed with the way you handled it, that I'll take you as my pupil. How much did you say you had?"

"Thirty dollars."

"I've got a friend who teaches a life drawing class. I'm going to ask him if he'll let you take it for your thirty dollars. I can't talk to you until you get more civilized."

"But thirty dollars is all the money I've got. I won't have anything left to pay you."

"I don't want your money. Take the class, and come see me when he tells you."

Diebold's friend, a guy named Schwartz, allowed me into his class. The students stood in front of easels, trying to draw a model, and Schwartz walked around smoking a cigar, and correcting our drawings. This is how he did it: he'd come up behind you, snatch the charcoal out of your hand, and mark up your drawing. He'd draw over your drawing to show where you'd gone wrong—gotten things out of proportion, or misconstrued a line.

Very soon I observed that when he'd come to correct me, just at the point when he was about to, or was in the act of snatching the charcoal, I would suddenly see, on the paper, where he was going to draw. I would anticipate what he was going to correct. I'd think, "Ah! I see what he's going to see!"

After a few weeks, Schwartz told me, "Go see Diebold. Bring your carving tools."

I went to see him.

"Schwartz says you've been coming to the drawing class," Diebold said. "You still want to study with me?"

"Sure."

"Then we have to discuss the terms of your apprenticeship," he said. "When will you be here?"

"Where?"

"Here. In this room."

"Well, I'm going to college. I have three months off in the summer, and two months in the winter."

"Fine. From this day forward, if you are in the city of Chicago, you are to walk through that door each morning as my bare feet touch the floor for the first time."

"Uh, what time of morning is that exactly?"

"Don't interrupt. You will appear first thing in the morning, and disappear when I tell you. The first day you miss, you're fired.

"I will be your teacher until you don't need me any more—or quit like a coward. Since it's impossible to teach art, I will teach you me. You just may pick up what you need to know. I also intend to confuse you severely. At times you may think you are losing your mind. If that happens, I will dive in and rescue you—but only as you're going down for the third time. Any questions?"

"Yes. Why do this for me?"

"I happen to think you might be worth it. Now get out your carving tools. I'm going to show you how to sharpen them. Pay attention, because this is the last time I will teach you anything directly."

That is how I began as the pupil of Navin Diebold, the product of whose teaching I am, for better or worse, to this day.

※ ※ ※

IN the days when I attended St. Leon's College they used to turn the students loose for a whole two months in the winter. The "Field Period," it was called, and we were supposed to do something useful, a job or an internship, or a research project, and write it up when we got back. A good idea, even if I did spend one of those field periods hanging out in a Greek restaurant in Chicago, and later tried to pass it off as research for a paper about changing mores in an immigrant community.

Because everybody was away in the months of January and February, the college started earlier than most and ran later—right to the end of June. This was regarded as a hardship by no one. The Hudson River valley, where the college was situated, and where I live today, is beautiful in June, and the college lands, formerly a great estate, included hundreds of acres of forest—much of it the work of nineteenth-century landscape architects, a simulated wilderness, with the occasional picturesque ruin.

In the middle of this carefully planned profusion of trees not native to the place, stone bridges going nowhere, and spectacular slopes of myrtle, a winding forest path led to a waterfall and, beside it, a concrete swimming pool.

In later years, a new sort of administration let the pool go to ruin—but when I was there, at least in the warm weather, it was at the center of daily life. Come June, we students dispensed with clothes, and strolled around in our bathrobes, with swimsuits underneath. Between classes, before lunch, and after supper, it was down the woodland path for a quick dip.

With swimming, lolling in the sun, inhaling the spring fragrance, the place took on the aspect of a summer camp or one of those Mediterranean-getaway resorts. People got silly and sensual about their studies, falling in love with Plato and Wallace Stevens—and one another. There was a good deal of wine-drinking and music in the evenings.

I need to say a little more about the character of this valley. It is beautiful. It is also mysterious, and a little scary at times. This is Ichabod Crane and Rip Van Winkle country. The native forests are dense and dark enough, and the artificial ones around St. Leon's, having been left to grow wild for a hundred years, are full of curious shapes and shadows as night comes on.

Light river mists would come up, sometimes an owl

would call, and on moonlit nights, the woods would be full of silver luminescence, dappled with shadows.

On a night like that I was returning from a swim. I was squelching up the path in my rubber shower sandals, in my robe, my damp towel draped over my neck. The path led to the edge of the woods, bordering a hillside meadow.

There I saw, running down the hill, a tiny woman, nude or nearly nude, trailing behind her some billowing filmy garments. I watched her as she descended the hill away from me, and into the trees. Very fleet she was. She ran easily, sometimes leaping like a deer.

In the moonlight, I couldn't tell if she was five feet tall, or three—a real woman or an apparition. Was it Diane Mitchell, who would be my girlfriend later that very summer—or a fairy?

❦ ❦ ❦

ONE of the Americans who won the Nobel Prize this year was Elias James Corey. He teaches at Harvard. Says here he helped to develop the theory and methodology of organic synthesis. The explanation for the rest of us says that means efficient methods for manufacturing plastics, synthetic fibers, dyes, and pharmaceutical products.

This is what he said when his students came celebrating to his office with cans of beer:

"This is a statistically improbable event," he said. "My philosophy has been to try to be as logical as I can. I try to teach my science."

There are still guys like that around. Spock lives.

I remember one semester in college when my friend George had run out of money. The physics professor invited him to come and live at his house for a semester.

One day, George said to me, "The professor and his wife are going out for the evening. They told me I could invite a friend over for coffee. So I'm inviting you."

I followed George's directions and walked through the woods, to a little house I'd never known was there. George was waiting for me. It was an extremely neat house.

"Let's make the coffee," George said. He got out one of those Chemex coffeepots, filter papers, a laboratory thermometer, and a logbook.

"It's a family experiment," George said. "To see if we can brew the perfect cup of coffee. We'll record the amount of ground coffee used, the temperature, and the duration of brewing. Also how many thicknesses of filter paper. After we drink the coffee, I'll have to ask you for your comments to enter in the log."

My comment was that they'd get better results if they used something other than the cheapest grade of A&P coffee.

It was a good college. Scientists were thrown together with artists a lot—unlike in the real world.

❧ ❧ ❧

WHEN I got to be a senior at St. Leon's College, I was given my very own studio. It was a tiny room in a creaky old wooden shedlike building. Here I was to work on my senior project, a series of woodblock prints.

I found, left behind by previous inhabitants, a dangerous electric percolator and a squawky old radio.

I loved having a studio of my own, and spent most of my time there. I'd arrive at ten or eleven at night and stay till dawn, chiseling away at my woodblocks, swilling black coffee, and listening to the all-night hillbilly station.

At sunrise I'd stroll to my room, where I would sleep

until lunchtime. I had signed up only for classes that met in the afternoon, and I had time in the evening to socialize and study before retiring to my little workshop.

The rest of the college would be sleeping when I was at work, and I had no distractions. I was getting a lot accomplished. It was an ideal routine, and I was happy.

It was during this period that the President of the United States was assassinated. Today, documentaries and news retrospectives emphasize the shock and grief felt by the nation—but I also remember the fear and confusion that closely followed the event.

At first it was unclear whether or not the assassination was part of a coup or insurrection. News reports were vague and fragmentary. There was speculation as to whether our country's enemies might not take advantage of the confusion of the moment and attack us. I hovered near the radio and learned of the capture of Oswald and later of his murder before the news cameras.

Lyndon Johnson had been sworn in as President. Harry S. Truman flew to Washington, and from the airport, broadcast a statement assuring the country that the orderly succession of government was intact. It was two or three days before the feeling of panic and uncertainty died down.

And the whole time, I was listening—while carving away at woodblocks, because there was nothing else to do. I was realizing that events can become ugly with a terrifying suddenness—and that I, personally, had nothing to contribute in times like these.

There were advisors in Southeast Asia. There was a wall in Berlin. We had nearly had a nuclear war over missiles in Cuba. People were being fire-hosed and police-dogged in the South. Now someone had knocked off the First Citizen of the Republic—and I was learning to do what? I was learning to make things for rich people to decorate their apartments with.

I felt useless and stupid. As the assassination hysteria subsided, I continued to come to the studio, but it seemed to me an empty exercise. Worse, a mockery. In times like these, the last thing needed was a little more art.

Then, one 2:00 A.M., a fellow student dropped in to see me. Jerry Schwartz was his name. I knew him by sight, but had never spoken with him. He had something to tell me.

It seemed Schwartz had gone through a period of living the life of a swine. He had been in the habit of coming home drunk at approximately the same time every morning. And every morning, he'd see the light in my studio, and through the window, me, doing . . . he didn't know what, but there I was doing it.

He felt that here was at least one person doing something probably constructive—anyway, functioning. It somehow meant to him that there was hope for him too.

In the parlance of Alcoholics Anonymous, the image of the light in my studio window had become his higher power, had kept him from despairing, motivated him to try to straighten out—and, as he told it, may have prevented his taking his own life.

I thought he was probably exaggerating, but I couldn't take the chance. Now I had to show up every night, and work on my woodcuts in order not to let down this formerly miserable Schwartz.

I didn't see Schwartz again, but I finished out the year and got my degree.

And gradually I became convinced that the best way I could address the big evils of the big world would be to keep chipping away at something comparatively small.

❧ ❧ ❧

I once found myself in Los Angeles during a winter break from college. I'd gotten an emergency call. My father, who was visiting in L.A., was dying. I took a plane. Who should meet me at the airport, in a rented convertible? My father.

"You look fine."

"Sure."

"They said you were dying."

"Not at dis time."

"So you're OK?"

"Relatively."

"Should you be driving around like this?"

"It's Los Angeles. You gotta drive."

"And your health . . . ?"

"Poifect."

"So what am I doing here?"

"It's nice here. You'll hev a vacation."

"Did you tell them to tell me you were dying?"

"I told *dem* I vas dying. I don' know vhat dey tol' you."

"When can I go home?"

"Vhen I tell you. You'll stay vit' your sister."

My father was staying at a hotel in Beverly Hills. I got to stay at my sister's house, where everybody got in cars and went about their business at six in the morning. I had no wheels, no money, and nothing to do.

I phoned a guy I'd known at college, an art major who had transferred to U.C.L.A.

"Mike, it's Pinkwater."

"You in town?"

"I'm stranded at my sister's house."

"Tell you what, I'll pick you up tonight. We'll go out."

"Swell."

Mike came to get me in a little sports car. He wanted to show me the work he was doing, so we drove over to the art school at U.C.L.A. I looked at his stuff. He was making portrait sculptures out of latex rubber.

"See, this way it feels like a real face."

I tweaked the nose of one of his portraits. "It feels like a rubber face."

Mike showed me around the studios. It was night, and nobody was there. I looked at various projects by various art students. There seemed to be a craze for mixed-media, collages, and odd materials—like Mike's rubber faces.

I came upon a large carton full of skulls.

"What's this?" I asked Mike.

"Skulls," Mike said. "Some guy dragged that box in here a few weeks ago. It's just been standing around."

"I've always wanted a skull. I'd like to keep it on my desk."

"So help yourself."

"Just take one?"

"Sure. He'll never miss it. Just shove it under your coat."

"Steal a skull?"

I did it.

I put the skull in the trunk, and we buzzed off to the movies. It was a midnight show—a double horror feature. After the pictures, we drove back to my sister's house.

Everybody was asleep. We tiptoed into the kitchen, and made coffee. The skull was on the kitchen table.

"Boy, this is neat," I said.

"Sure is," Mike said.

"I didn't just take it for trivial reasons," I said.

"Not at all," Mike said. "Art students need skulls."

I was noticing that it wasn't one of those anatomist's skulls that have been boiled in paraffin, and are white and neat-looking. This one was a lead-grey color. The teeth were loose, and every time I moved it, a little cone of powdery clay would fall out of the foramen magnum. It had been dug up somewhere.

"You know . . . this is somebody's head," I told Mike.

"I was just thinking the same thing."

"You wouldn't want to take it . . . back, would you?"

"Can't take the risk, pal. I'm enrolled there. If they found me skipping around with someone else's skull they could expel me."

Throwing it into the garbage was out of the question, and just dumping it somewhere in the neighborhood was equally unacceptable. It wasn't the sort of thing that could be overlooked if found—there could be trouble—and besides, it was part of a former person.

It went back to New York in my suitcase.

I was stuck with it. The mandible kept breaking, and I'd patch it with Elmer's Glue. It looked like I'd have to keep the thing until it finished decomposing.

Then I went to visit my friend George.

"I got a skull when I was out in Los Angeles," I said.

"Really? I've always wanted a skull," George said.

"Tell you what, you can have mine."

"No fooling?"

"On one condition. You can't give it back."

"Why should I want to give it back?"

"Just you can't, agreed?"

I ran and got George the skull. I left while he was still happy with it. The next day, he called me on the phone.

"This thing is horrible."

"I know."

"Take it back."

"We made a deal. You don't like it, get rid of it."

"How? I can't just throw it out with the garbage."

"I know."

George had the skull for a long time. It sat moldering on the shelf in his closet. When he got married, his wife came to live in his apartment. First thing she did was tidy up the place. She got rid of odd socks, old magazines, outdated yogurt from the back of the refrigerator—and she found the skull.

"This is nasty," she said, and dropped it down the chute to the incinerator.

My father asked me, "So vhat did you finally did vit' that skull?"

"I gave it to my friend George."

"And vhat did he did vit' it?"

"His wife threw it out."

"Yeh. Vhen you get married, you should pick a smart goil too."

❧ ❧ ❧

WINTER and summer, for three years, I underwent the experience of being the apprentice of Navin Diebold. Each morning, I appeared at his studio, whereupon he would look at me quizzically, as though he had never seen me before or there were something awry or unbuttoned about my clothes. He would remain silent, his gaze fixed upon me, waiting.

"Good morning," I would say. "What would you like me to do today?"

There were usually a number of projects—his and mine—going on at once in the studio. I enjoyed it when he would let me do the rough work on something of his. He allowed this rarely, and only when there was a material or technical problem involved that I had not experienced before.

Sometimes I would sit and watch him work—sometimes he would sit and watch me work. I don't recall a time when we were both concentrating on separate things.

44

"Do? Anything you like."

I would then begin to scour the studio for clues. At times, Diebold would have arranged all my tools in a circle, the points directed to the center, in which sat a hunk of wood. Or I might find all those pieces of mine that were unfinished and unresolved failures, placed on the floor, in a serpentine pattern, leading like stepping stones from the door where I would enter, to the carving table.

There were also daily bulletins, cryptic notes in Magic Marker, posted on the walls. "Why is limestone when it spins?" one might say. Or, "Describe negative space without using any negatives," or "Have you taken your Dynamic Symmetry?" or "Pinkwater is a big fat pussycat." From all these playful indicators, I would try to figure out what Diebold wanted me to do.

When I asked him a direct question of a technical nature, he would hurl a book at my head. "Look it up!" he would shout, as I dodged or caught the copy of *Materials and Methods of Sculpture*, by Jack C. Rich. "I am not a book!"

After a while, I would figure out what task he had subtly set for me, and go about it.

I must have been studying with him for a year and a half when it finally occurred to me to ask him, "You know how I come in here every morning, and ask you what you want me to do?"

"Yes."

"And every morning, you say I should do whatever I like?"

"Yes."

"And then for the next half hour, I try to figure out those Zen puzzles you set up during the night?"

"Yes."

"They don't mean anything, do they?"

"No."

"And when you say I can do whatever I like, you mean

that I can do whatever I like. I can work. I can watch you work. I can take a nap. I can look out the window, get drunk, read a magazine, eat my lunch, play your records, yodel, hold my breath. I can discuss Mozart with you, or get you to try to teach me to fence. I can invite my friends in and have a party."

"Only if you know some pretty girls."

"So, actually, when you say I can do anything I like, you simply, literally, mean that I can do anything I like."

"I say so every day."

"I'll be damned."

"And that was the first lesson. You know, if you take this long to figure everything out, you'll still be my apprentice when you're ninety."

🐝 🐝 🐝

I USED to know all about Zen Buddhism. In fact, I was a sort of walking encyclopedia of Zen. I had read all the Zen books. I gave a report on Zen in a class in college, and got an A for it. At the drop of a hat, I would explain Zen to anyone who would listen.

My teacher, Navin Diebold, would not listen. I thought as an artist and a sensitive person, he would be especially interested, but he wasn't. Every time I tried to explain Zen to him, he'd deftly change the subject.

"Look," I finally said to him. "If I gave you something to read, would you read it?"

"Sure," Navin Diebold said. "I like to read."

One of the things I knew about Zen—and it turns out to have been the only thing I knew that was so—was which book about Zen was the best. It's a book called *Zen Flesh, Zen Bones*, by Paul Reps and Nyogen Sazaki. It contains traditional Zen stories—like this:

A man is being chased by a tiger, and comes to the edge of a precipice. So he jumps over, and saves himself from falling all the way by catching hold of a root. Hanging there, he sees there's another tiger at the bottom of the cliff. Then he notices that a couple of mice are gnawing at the base of the root he's holding on to. Nearby, there's a single strawberry growing. So what does he do? He eats the strawberry—and how sweet it tastes!

Another one tells about two monks arguing about a flag.

One says "The flag is moving."

The other says, "The wind is moving."

An enlightened type happens by and corrects them both. "Not the wind, not the flag—mind is moving."

There are a lot of other stories, a good deal of discussion of the sound made by one hand clapping, and if you read the whole thing, you get a pretty good taste of Zen.

I brought the book to Diebold and sat quietly while he read it—for a whole rainy afternoon. He sat in the window, reading the book, smoking mentholated cigarettes.

I sat in the armchair, waiting for him to finish. Then we could have a good discussion. I was prepared to answer any questions he might have.

Diebold read the last page. He tossed the book onto the day bed.

"Well?" I asked him. "What do you think?"

"Hell of a thing," he said. "I've been a Zen Master all this time, and I didn't even know it."

NAVIN Diebold had a girlfriend, Lydia. She was nice to me.

"That guy is hard to put up with," I told her.

"You're telling me. Try being his girlfriend."

"It couldn't be worse than being his apprentice. Why does he have to bend my mind all the time?"

"Listen. He takes you very seriously. You know what he did?"

"What?"

"When you first asked him to teach you—before he even told you he would—he fired all his other students."

"He had other students?"

"Housewives from the suburbs. He'd hold their hands and tell them they were talented. It was the only steady income he had."

"And he fired them?"

"He told me he had to concentrate on teaching you."

"I never knew that."

"Yeah. Well."

"Wow."

About the time I graduated from college, Diebold told me that my apprenticeship was over.

"You mean I'm an artist?"

"No, I mean your apprenticeship is over."

The summer before, he'd told me, "Get a show."

"Get a show?"

"Why do I always have to explain everything? Get your drawings and woodcuts and whatnot together, and get a show—so the public can see your work."

"You think I'm ready for that?"

"You most decidedly are not ready—but it's time you got your feet wet. Otherwise, later, you'll get all neurotic."

By this time, it had become my practice to do everything he told me, only more so. I got *three* shows. The most successful one was in an arty saloon, where every piece was sold. The bartender was big and strong, and when drunks wrote on my drawings, he'd make them buy them.

Now that I was done being an apprentice, and was

through with college, I had a surprise for my teacher. I was going to stick around, look after him, take care of him in his old age. He was then about three years younger than I am today, but I saw him as decrepit. I got a studio in the same building, and told him that supper was organized every night until further notice.

"Don't you want to go to New York and crack the art world?" he asked me.

"I'm fine right here, Navin," I told him. "It's spaghetti with clam sauce tonight."

So every night, Navin Diebold would come up to my place and eat his supper, and glimpse at what I was working on.

The next day, when I'd get lonely and drop down to his place to hang out, I'd find, already finished, something that successfully resolved whatever problem was resisting me upstairs. He wasn't making the same sculptures as I was—he was making better ones that did the same thing.

"Look, I don't want you coming up to my studio anymore," I said.

"Fine by me," Diebold said.

"I'll bring your supper down to you."

"Whatever you say."

The next morning, I could hear muffled tapping coming from Diebold's studio when I first opened my eyes. I started work on a new piece, and stayed with it all day. When I brought Diebold his supper, he was just finishing a new piece of his own—just like mine, only it worked.

For the next couple of weeks, he managed to stay ahead of me, even though he couldn't see what I was doing. I tried radically changing my direction a couple of times, but he anticipated that. The devil knew my every thought.

So I decided to move to New York. Crack the art world. I bought an old car, and loaded all my stuff into it.

The night before I left, I went to see Diebold.

"You about ready to go?"

"All packed."

"Well, there are two things I want to say to you before you go."

"Yes?"

"Yes. I've enjoyed being your teacher. Now I want to tell you that you will never be a sculptor."

"What?"

"A sculptor. Guy who makes statues and that. You won't be one. I never thought you would."

I sputtered for a while. "What a creepy thing to say! What do you mean? I *am* a sculptor!"

"No you're not—and you'll never be one."

"Oh yeah? Then why did you spend three years teaching me all this stuff?"

"I was never interested in what kind of artist you were going to be. I was interested in what kind of man you were going to be. You want to know what you're going to wind up doing?"

"What?"

"You're going to be a writer."

"A writer! I don't want to be a writer! Everybody tells me I'm going to be a writer! Writers are sissies! They sit around, bending over typewriters, polluting the atmosphere with bunches of unnecessary words. They get eyestrain and backache and coffee nerves and typist's elbow. To hell with that! I'm going to get a loft in Brooklyn, or maybe move up around Woodstock, and knock out huge wood sculptures, and marry a fat woman, and get stuff in the Whitney Museum. You're crazy!"

"All the same. You're going to be a writer."

"Great. Fine. What was the other thing you wanted to tell me?"

"Don't tell anybody who you studied with."

"Have I ever told you that you have a sick sense of humor?"

"Often."

As I walked out of Diebold's studio, I heard him say softly, maybe to himself, "Fly, fly, birdie. Out of the nest."

❧ ❧ ❧

So there I was, having graduated from St. Leon's College, with a degree in art. What to do next? I decided to go back to Chicago, and look for a job.

There was nothing in the classifieds under "S" for sculptor or "A" for artist. However, I did find something under "W" for woodcarver.

It turned out that the job consisted of carving various ornamental thingamajigs out of wood—mirror frames, cuckoo-clock fronts, little scenes. The carvings would be used to make molds that would be injected with a liquid plastic with particles of sawdust suspended in it, which would harden into a woodlike plastic or a plasticlike wood. Pay for a beginner was sixty dollars a week.

Some of the big customers for this kind of thing were motel chains, I was told. I was also told that I was not being offered the job.

"It's just that you're so old to be starting in this trade," Mike, the boss, said. "Most of our workers are from Europe, they started when they were twelve—and you're what, twenty-one?"

About a week later Mike called me up. "Nobody else applied for the job," he said. "I still have reservations about hiring you, but maybe your having gone to college will make up for the late start. Come in Monday."

I had to bring my own carving tools, a clean shop coat, and a stool to sit on. The workbench was provided.

There were five or six other carvers, all from Hungary. Janos was the foreman. I never saw Mike the boss again.

"You gonna want pastry?" Janos said. "Costs two-fifty a week with coffee too. Good pastry."

I signed on for the pastry.

Big windows opened onto the factory across the street, where Milk Duds were manufactured. About every fifteen minutes, a vent would open somewhere in that factory and let out a fragrant cloud of the smell of that candy sold in movie houses, and which no one has ever seen in full illumination. These periodic whiffs made me ravenous for something sweet.

At 10:30 A.M. somebody came in with a box of truly devastating pastries. Hungarians are very advanced about this kind of thing. The old woodcarvers and I would knock off for a few minutes and drink rich coffee and eat pastry that was never the same, except that it was always like heaven.

Janos had assigned me the *Niña*, *Pinta*, and *Santa Maria*.

"Make them, oh, about this size—in low relief, all right?"

Janos handed me a sketch that had come up from the Art Department. It was nothing but a smudge. If it hadn't been labeled *Niña*, *Pinta*, and *Santa Maria*, it might as well have been the Three Kings, or Groucho, Harpo, and Zeppo.

Janos saw that I was perplexed, and directed me to an extensive library—books the men had brought from home. They used these to make up the appalling deficiencies of the Art Department. If an order came up for winter roses, accompanied by the usual shmear of a drawing, one of the Janoses would find an illustration and adapt it to a carving.

I found a suitable picture to work from and sketched the famous ships.

"So you guys really design this stuff," I said to Janos.

"Oh no, just simple carvers," he said. "We wouldn't know what to make if the bosses didn't tell us."

I got to work on Columbus's ships, inhaling Milk Dud fumes, and dreaming of tomorrow's pastry. The old guys worked in silence. The only sound in the place was the precise chipping of their sharp tools. Everyone was working on different projects, but I could tell the others were about three times as fast as I was.

By Friday, I had gotten through the three ships, and my carvings had been taken off to be transformed into many multiples of injection-molded lifelike plastic. Perhaps my work has given you enjoyment during a stay at some Econo-Lodge.

Janos handed me my pay envelope. "You not doing so bad," he said. "You got talent. You stay with it, maybe in a few years you make ninety dollars a week, like Janos."

Monday, I got my new assignment—an ass eating thistles. A suffocating feeling came over me.

"I quit," I said.

"Why quit?" Janos asked.

"I can't stand this. I can't stand carving these dopey things."

"But you got ability. Why you want to waste it?"

"I want to make my own stuff," I said.

"Oho! You an artist! A real sculptor!" Janos said.

The other woodcarvers nodded respectfully as I walked down the row of benches, with my roll of tools and my stool—never again to use my skill as a bondslave of commerce—anyway, not at those prices.

⁂

HERE'S the other reason I left Chicago and moved to New York. My studio was located on the south side of North Avenue, a couple of blocks west of Welles Street. The neighborhood, known as Old Town, has long been

Chicago's artistic district. There were galleries, funky saloons favored by poets and painters, and a fair amount of bearded or batiked, sandaled sensitives in residence.

There was also an influx of tourists from the suburbs, evenings and weekends. Just down the street, someone had opened a sort of arcade wherein one could have one's caricature drawn by a real beatnik, purchase crude jewelry on a leather thong, or create a real work of abstract art.

One did this by paying a dollar for the privilege of squirting paint out of plastic catsup bottles at a square of spinning paper stuck to a turntable at the bottom of a cylindrical drum. Spin-Art, I believe it's called—still featured at county fairs—it was a new idea then.

The result was a sort of centrifugal mandala, lacelike colors, webbing out from the center. The finished products would be handed to the clients, still wet—and they would carry them to their cars held flat, like trays.

We were a couple of years from the psychedelic explosion. In San Francisco, the Haight-Ashbury was still nothing more than a crummy neighborhood. This was the first whiff of the new taste. The official art world was teetering between the fourth (or was it fifth?) generation of abstract expressionism and Pop and Op. I knew this because I'd recently been to New York. In Chicago, no territory beyond Jackson Pollack had yet been discovered.

I'd gotten into Navin Diebold's habit of leaning out my window evenings, and watching the nightly procession of pub crawlers, tourists, and beatniks. While doing this— the equivalent of viewing tropical fish—I'd think over the pressing problems of my young life.

Besides the obvious ones—connected with my having nothing better to do than stare out the window—there was the question of where I would take my stand as a newly graduated artist. Should I follow in the tradition of Diebold, my teacher, who had gone down some stylistic

side-road in the late 1940s, ensuring obscurity forever-
more?

Or, should I abandon ethics and pursue the synthetic
schools that were being promoted in New York, and try my
luck as an Opper or Popper? And if I did, wasn't there a
strong possibility that I'd be too late?

Or should I follow my personal muse, and simply make
what Art I needs must make, ignoring the fads and fancies
of a shallow world? Trouble was, there wasn't really any
evidence that I was acquainted with a personal muse—or
even somebody else's muse. Like a lot of people who study
art, I hadn't given a moment's thought to the possibility
that, come to it, I might have nothing to say.

And while I was thinking these things over, down below
me, in the street, was an endless procession of those
squares of paper, being carried like holy relics. Hundreds,
nay thousands, of fresh, still-wet Spin-Arts, meaningless
circles and sunbursts bobbing under the streetlights, on
their way to adorn walls in Skokie, Winnetka, and Lin-
colnwood.

I realized something—a thought suppressed until now.
Those damn things were better than the stuff I was doing!

I bought a 1959 Peugeot station wagon with four good
tires, and took off for New York one foggy night, the lights
of Chicago making a spiderwebby aurora behind me.

※ ※ ※

WHEN you want to leave a message for ages yet
unborn, you make it in 3-D and out of something hard.
Paintings are handy for patching the roof, manuscripts
give comforting heat when burned, and poems are made
by fools like some who are reading at this moment. If you

want to be sure that your contribution to culture has a chance of being appreciated much, much later—hack it out of granite.

So it is that students of sculpture always make friends with the distant past. Your Egyptian or Sumerian stone-whacker employed tools and methods pretty much identical to those of the modern exponent of the art, and no doubt had many of the same problems. When you spend your days making graven, or cast, or hammered-together images, you start to feel kinship with these old dead guys.

Thus, as a young rock-bopper, I visited the art museums a lot, but no less the museums of ethnology. My favorite haunts were the Brooklyn Museum—a special treasure with its halls of Pacific Northwest Indian and African and Oceanic art—and the American Museum of Natural History, which has ten of everything the Brooklyn's got—but not displayed as well.

And there was one other place—in its way better than either museum—a shop on the West Side of Manhattan, called the House of Antiquities. This place sold to the public artifacts that were completely authentic, but not of museum quality.

The various dynasties of Egypt left behind as many scarabs and faience beads as we will leave Coke bottles. Likewise, earthenware lamps—the little pitcherlike jobs— were the light bulbs of the ancient world, and frangible as they are, enough survived that the House of Antiquities could make a profit selling them at seven or eight bucks a time.

Of course, the appeal of this shop was that you could handle everything, and even take it home with you, if you desired. It was a little hole-in-the-wall in a bad neighborhood. You'd ring the bell—they'd unlock the door. In attendance was not some desiccated scholar, but a friendly, zaftig woman of the Bronx—the best kind— whose enthusiasm and informality made the experience even more like visiting a shop in Rome or Constantinople in the very old days. I think her name was Edith.

Everything I bought there, I have since given away—some bronze Byzantine rings, a set of arrowheads from Amlash, an eighteenth-century Siamese Buddha, a Ptolmaic coin with a wonderful head of Zeus, his hair and whiskers curling everywhere—that piece I kept the longest, carrying it in my pocket for years.

It was there in the House of Antiquities that I tasted a mummy case.

Edith had gone into the back to answer the phone, or fetch some additional artifacts to show me, and I was scrutinizing this very nice mummy case—not special—like everything in the place—just a good example of a late dynastic, wooden, gessoed, and polychromed box in good condition. The lid was off and stood beside the thing. The interior painting was in fine shape. One of the edges was chipped, revealing an inch or two of plain wood, very smooth with tiny wormholes.

I'd been looking the object up and down, touching it lightly, turning the lid around to look at the painting on the other side, and now—I tasted the wood. I had and have no idea why. I touched the tip of my tongue to that chipped spot.

It was *not* an inconclusive experience. I felt an electric jolt that went right down to my heels. For a hundredth of a second I thought I felt a blast of hot, dry air, and may have glimpsed or almost glimpsed a sky and horizon illuminated by a sun that had not shone for millennia.

The only physical experience I remember that was comparable was the time my brother gave me a pinch of powdered pit viper, which some Asians use as a tonic.

Edith returned, and perceiving my expression, gave herself away as a fellow mummy taster.

"What did you do?" she asked accusingly.

"I tasted the mummy case."

"Never do that!" she said. "You don't know what sort of chemicals they used on those things!"

"I read somewhere that in the Middle Ages, they'd take ground-up mummy as medicine."

"Well, keep your tongue in your mouth around here," Edith said. "That mummy case is dynamite."

You see, that's why the shop was superior to a museum in many ways. You can't learn a thing by licking the glass at the Natural History.

HOBOKEN
NIGHTS

ONE of the great things about Hoboken was that it looked at New York across the Hudson River. Even modest, low-rent dwellings in Hoboken might command a spectacular view of the Manhattan skyline. From my second loft in Hoboken I could see from just below the George Washington Bridge to Staten Island, with a sliver of Brooklyn visible, and all the shipping in the harbor.

Close as it was to the big town—it was a place apart. A refuge.

After a day of trying to crack the Art World, I could take the swift Hudson Tubes, a secret subway known only to the few, or the majestic steam-powered Barclay Street ferry, to Hoboken where life was gracious. Well, not gracious—but sustainable.

From the ferry docks, I could look across the river, shimmering with lights reflected from the tall buildings, and say, "I'm clear of you, monster. Stay there, while I recharge my batteries."

Hoboken had a pace and a style all its own. It was in decline when I came there—but there was plenty of evidence of the vital little city it had been. With cliffs to the north—the Palisades—and marshland to the south, it had been the only natural port on the Jersey side of the Hudson, and all traffic to and from the west had passed through it in the old days.

In the eighteenth century, New Yorkers would row or sail across to Hoboken to visit picnic groves, taverns, gaming parlors, and other sorts of parlors. It was just across the town line in Weehawken where Aaron Burr and Alexander Hamilton went to have their duel.

In the nineteenth and twentieth centuries, much transatlantic shipping originated in Hoboken. Fashionable travelers would stay a day or two in hotels, visiting theaters and beer gardens while their lighterage was being transferred to the ship. And all the troops heading for Europe in World War One left from Hoboken, and returned there, the origin of the expression "Hell or Hoboken by Christmas."

Charles Dickens lived in Hoboken for a while in 1842. Stephen Foster wrote "Jeanie with the Light Brown Hair" there. And Edgar Allan Poe based "The Mystery of Marie Roget" on a local murder case.

Marconi either invented the wireless there, or lived there after he invented it. Anyway, he lived there. The first professional baseball game was played in Hoboken. The zipper was invented in Hoboken, and the first ice cream cone, it is said.

There were frequent flowerings of culture in Hoboken. Periodically, it would be discovered by a new bunch of artists and writers looking for cheap digs and linguine with clam sauce.

The movie *On the Waterfront* was shot there.

The musical *Hair* was written there.

And there was a big sign on the side of the Clam Broth House stating that Frank Sinatra had been born there.

The main drag, Washington Street, had wide pavements once dark with crowds of lunch-hour shoppers who came over from lower Manhattan on the ferries. Fancy emporiums stood empty or deserted. Saloons now catering to a handful of neighborhood regulars were huge and ornate, if a little tarnished and dusty. Once they had been packed with customers lifting schooners of beer, and making use of the free-lunch counter—an institution that, I'm happy to say, had not entirely died out when I arrived.

A few old-timers still spoke in the old Hoboken accent—with elements of Boston Irish and Down East Maine, and a tiny hint of Popeye the Sailor Man.

I loved that town. Every street, every block contained some relic or curiosity to be discovered. But the greatest thing about Hoboken was the people who lived there, the magnificent array of characters and types. I'll tell you about some of them—another time.

※ ※ ※

HERMAN Hermann, the art-supplies dealer, was more than that. He was a friend and advisor to young artists, and he made himself useful to the big guys. Salvador Dali was a steady client of his. He'd drag blocks of paper and stretched canvases over to the Maestro's place on his little express wagon. They spoke the same language—Surrealist.

Herman Hermann resembled Matisse—also my father. It was he who was responsible for my discovery of Hoboken—my favorite place on earth.

I was trying to work and live in a fifth-floor rat farm on Twenty-fourth Street. It was unsatisfactory.

"Herman, I need a loft," I said. For purposes of this discussion, loft means studio. It would be an elderly commercial or manufacturing space made over into a dwelling. There were basically two kinds of lofts, legal and illegal. The illegal ones you weren't supposed to live in, and you'd have to keep your bed in a packing crate labeled "Live Vipers" to fool the fire inspector, and do without heat on weekends. The legal ones tended to cost a lot, plus bribes and key money.

"I know of a loft," Herman Hermann said. "But you have to like music." Herman Hermann, like my father, was given to enigmatic remarks. He might as well have said, "But you have to like shredded wheat." It was, I assumed, an inexplicable saying, such as he was fond of making. Some things he said over and over, and seldom did they become clear. "In 1959 I ate a bowl of that macrobiotic rice, and every rice was like a bullet." Was that good or bad? I never found out.

"So go to Hoboken. See the local magistrate, Judge Amadeo. He'll fix you up."

I found my way to Hoboken, New Jersey, right across the Hudson from New York. A subway went there. When I emerged out of the ground, I fell instantly and deeply in love.

What met my gaze was a huge ship at anchor. Seagulls wheeling overhead. Steam-powered ferryboats toiling back and forth. Curiously ornamented buildings. A great, green, copper-fronted railway station. A cobblestone street. My God! It was an old port, hardly changed in eighty or a hundred years. All of this bathed in golden September sunshine.

I thought I could smell the sea mixed in with river. A huge neon sign, depicting a hand with index finger extended, pointed down, like the hand of God, at the original Clam Broth House—where steamer clams good enough for God to eat were served in massive buckets.

Guys built like fireplugs rolled up and down the pavements. Packards and Studebakers and DeSotos were parked at the curbs. The Goodyear blimp was passing overhead. It was a time warp. Everything that did not bespeak the nineteenth century was at least prewar. What a place!

I found Judge Amadeo in his office. He had silver hair, a neat moustache, and wore pinstripe trousers. A gray fedora hung on the coat tree.

The loft, it turned out, had once been a drill hall for some local militia, and a clandestine dance hall and blind pig during prohibition. It had smooth hardwood floors, steam heat, thirteen-foot ceilings, twenty-two hundred square feet. The rent was sixty dollars a month.

Some of the windows looked at other windows, and

some looked out over the rooftops of Hoboken, and out to New York Harbor and the sea. You could see the Statue of Liberty.

"I like artists," Judge Amadeo said. "My wife and I often spend a Sunday afternoon at the Metropolitan Museum of Art. If you decide to rent the loft, I'll come by on Saturday, and get everything working in the bathroom and kitchen—you see, before I became a lawyer, I was a plumber. I grew up here. I know the people who live here and I love most of them. If anybody gives you trouble, say you met me."

I spent the day walking the streets of Hoboken, burping clam sauce, and marveling at the town, the quaint architecture, and the more quaint citizens. Maybe a little crummy, but beautiful, it was to be my home for the next dozen years, and my spiritual home for the rest of my life.

What came to pass in Hoboken, what I learned and who I met, my brushes with the underworld, and how I came to appreciate and understand the meaning of culture, and why I still can't stand Puerto Rican music— The reader will discover later on.

☸ ☸ ☸

THE first thing I saw that made me want to live in Hoboken was the ferryboats. Owned by the Erie Lackawanna railroad, they crossed the Hudson between Hoboken, and Barclay Street in lower Manhattan. Built in the last century, the two oldest ones were steam driven, with tall smokestacks.

Trim and graceful, with sweeping rounded lines, they did not resemble floating apartment houses like the monsters that travel to Staten Island. They were paneled within. The varnish on the mahogany had checkered and crazed, but there was still a quality of graciousness. Handsome staircases connected the upper and lower decks, and there were places one could stand outside, and feel the weather during the crossing.

For those within, there were large plate glass windows, to view the river traffic and the New York skyline. During the age to which the ferries properly belonged, bankers and stockbrokers would alight from trains connecting to elegant suburbs in New Jersey, pick up their *Wall Street Journal*, and enjoy a coffee and a morning cigar on board.

In my day, you could still get a first-rate frankfurter, or a hot pretzel in the station, and carry it onto the ferry. Every day, I'd knock off work in my studio at noon, and ride back and forth. Sometimes back and forth and back and forth. You could ride as many times as you wanted for your quarter, and sometimes a fine spring afternoon would lengthen into evening, and I'd still be on the water. Few people still used the ferry, and often I'd have the boat almost to myself.

The ferry would churn out of the slip in Hoboken, directly across from Fourteenth Street, and out into the middle of the river. Then it would turn its blunt nose to the south, and travel along the commercial wharves, nosing in at Barclay Street, a few blocks from City Hall, and Wall Street.

Torn down to make way for nothing in particular was the old Washington Market, block after block of fruit and vegetable dealers, cheese factors, coffee roasters, the entire pistachio nut industry, and some of the oldest and finest commercial architecture in New York. Also nearby was Radio Row, tube, and later transistor, heaven, and no end of specialist hardware stores, and ship's chandlers, rope makers, places that sold scientific and philosophical instruments. It was like taking the day boat to Oz.

The only thing that could have made it better would have been to have some official connection with those marvelous boats. Every week for a period of years, I called the employment office at the railroad to find out if an opening for a deckhand on the ferry had occurred. The job consisted of wielding a mop, and latching and unlatching the gates. Of course some hundreds of other beatniks preceded me on the waiting list, and besides, who'd quit a job like that?

It was the ferry that quit. In the late sixties, it was announced that on a certain day the Barclay Street–Hoboken ferry would make its last run.

All the last week I rode the ferry every day, taking pictures. On the last day, I was aboard from noon to the last crossing. As evening came on, the ferry became crowded. People brought champagne on board, and there were two jazz bands. For once, the ferry looked and felt something as it might have in its glory days. The crew invited passengers to come below and see the mighty steam engine, clean and shining as the day it was built, smoothly and effortlessly sending the great boat through the dark water.

The very last crossing. Confetti. Drinks handed all round. The New York City fireboats shooting streams of water into the sky, and every horn and bell on the river sounding. Red distress flares lighting up the night.

We pulled into the Hoboken slip singing "Auld Lang Syne"—and then—the passengers trashed the boat. Anything made of brass was wrenched loose. Hundreds of orange kapok-filled life jackets were carried off. Seats were pried up. I actually saw a middle-aged woman walking off the ramp carrying the ship's wheel.

I stood around for a while, watching some people

working a newel post off the staircase. Then I grabbed a life preserver, and headed for home, pondering the mutability of human affections and the relentlessness of history.

※ ※ ※

THE loft I rented in Hoboken was an enormous thing. It was a single room, eighty-eight feet long, twenty-five feet wide, and thirteen feet high. It had good strong floors, and plenty of windows. A dream studio. Rumor had it that Hans Hoffmann and Willem De Kooning might have occupied it years past—but I doubt that either of them could have been responsible for the interior decor.

It was painted a ghastly, devastating, deep coral pink. Not a color I wanted to live with. I envisioned it all white.

"Just go ahead and paint it," Judge Amadeo, my landlord, told me. "I'll pay for the paint. Twenty gallons should do it."

Painting that room would be equivalent to doing over a good-sized yacht turned inside out, and I had never painted anything.

My family raised me to be completely useless as a do-it-yourselfer. I was not given a junior carpenter's kit as a little kid. And when I got a D double minus in woodshop in junior high, nobody at home seemed to mind.

This was a prejudice of my father's that he imposed on me. For all I knew, he had built the ship he came over on— and his horny, calloused hands suggested that he'd done plenty of manual labor. But now those hands were manicured every week, and never did anything more technical than change a light bulb.

Not only was I discouraged from engaging in domestic crafts, I was forbidden to own blue jeans, lest I be taken for a common laborer, and shame him.

I finally got to indulge in the pleasure of making things when I became an art major in college—about which my father had certain reservations. "I didn't valk helfway across Europe det you should vork vit' your hends," he said.

All I knew about painting I had to extrapolate from my course in oil painting, and a few odd words of advice from Judge Amadeo and the guy at the paint store.

I enlisted various friends to help me. Such friends as I had. Ken Kelman spent an entire day painting a radiator with a one-inch brush, never getting a single spot on his gabardine slacks or sport jacket, and when he was done, wanted me to take a photo of the radiator. His childhood was exactly like mine. After the radiator, Kelman got bored and went away.

But I, the intended inhabitant of the loft, had to make progress or live for years in an enormous pink room with one white corner and a white radiator. I learned as I went. I had fifty-two hundred square feet to do—and it was going to take two coats to cover that roseate atrociousness.

It took a week. I scampered up and down ladders. I mastered the roller and the brush. I did the window frames in gloss enamel. Gradually, the room took on a wonderful brilliance, and silence—the whiteness of a blizzard.

I became a demon painter. For years after, I would volunteer to paint my friends' apartments. I could do an average New York City dwelling in two hours. "Go to the movies," I'd say. "When you come back it'll be done."

The week I painted my Hoboken loft I remember as pure pleasure and triumph. Of course, I was only there during hours of daylight. When twilight came, I'd spend a little time surveying my work, drop in at the Clam Broth House for a bucket of steamers, and head for Manhattan, where I was bunking with a friend.

I had never been in the loft at night. I knew nothing of the strange events, the accursed happenings, the chaos and madness that awaited me.

🦋 🦋 🦋

Ron Brown lived in the loft upstairs in Hoboken. He was a painter and a perfectionist. His life was a constant struggle against flaws and untidiness.

When Ron bought a pair of shoes, he would wear them in the house for several days, covered by plastic bags, while he decided if the fit was precise.

When he bought a television, no fewer than fourteen ostensibly identical sets from two different dealers were delivered, unpacked, inspected, and returned until he found one that suited him.

Ron was shy and reclusive. Few people had seen his paintings, but those who had said they were marvelous. Once, Ron agreed to let an art dealer see his work, but at the last minute decided the paintings were not ready. He told the gallery man through the closed door that his mother was not home, and that he had been told not to allow anyone in.

When I'd known Ron for about a year, he invited me to see his work.

What I saw was incredible. While modern in style and content, they were paintings from another age, executed with a kind of precision and care beyond anything I'd ever seen.

"All these stars are painted with a one-hair brush," he said. "And each of them has to be painted three times."

Ron disliked texture. The surface of the pictures was as

smooth, as clear, as air. There were no brush-strokes. The paint was utterly flat. Color abutted color seamlessly. I saw powerful lenses and eye loupes among his tools. The paint had been laid on these canvases at a distance of one inch and at four times magnification.

The craft was lapidary—but the pictures were not small in any way. They were big, and forceful, and violent, and really like magic.

All of one wall was taken up with large sheets of paper, a preliminary cartoon for an enormous painting. After an hour, he switched off the light, and we left the studio. It was the only time I was ever allowed in.

But I discovered that if I leaned far out the window of my bathroom, which was set at an angle to Ron's windows, I could see through a window of his studio, and get a view of the wall with the huge sketch on it. Thus, I was able to watch the progress of that picture.

Ron told me he was building a stretcher—that's the wooden framework to which the canvas is affixed—some twelve by twenty-five feet in size. (He didn't know that I'd been spying through his window and watching the sketch take form.)

He selected kiln-dried oak to build the stretcher. Naturally, several shipments of lumber had to be sent back because he discovered slight warpage and irregularities of grain. When the thing was finished, it was a masterpiece of carpentry. Made the right way, with turnbuckles, it was beautiful enough to hang in a museum as it was.

Next was the canvas. Ron only used a special extra-fine-weave Belgian linen. He went to Herman Hermann, the art supplies dealer.

"A piece that size has to be special-ordered from the mill," Herman Hermann said. "It'll cost a lot, and they won't be able to make it until December."

Fine. Ron paid in advance, and went home to wait six months for his canvas.

On a dark January day, Ron knocked on my door.

"May I borrow your station wagon? My canvas has arrived. Herman Hermann just called."

This is what happened when Ron Brown arrived at Herman Hermann's shop.

"Where's my canvas?" he asked.

"Right here," Herman Hermann said, kicking a large bundle.

"It's in a bunch? On the floor?"

"What did you expect? Neatly rolled? It's twelve feet wide. This is how they shipped it."

"It's dirty."

"Yeh. It's a dirty floor."

"I can't accept this."

"It's yours. You paid for it. If you want another piece it'll take a year, and I assure you, it'll come the same way."

"But it's all creased."

Ron finally bundled the canvas into the car, and brought it home.

He stapled it to the masterpiece stretcher. Then he had occasion to telephone Herman Hermann.

"The canvas . . ."

"Yes?"

"It's got a big stain. A ring. Brown. As though somebody put a gallon can of varnish or something on it."

"So?"

"How am I supposed to paint on that?"

"Look. You're going to prime that canvas with gesso, made of equal parts plaster, whiting, and rabbit-skin glue, right? Then you're going to put down two coats of white lead, right?"

"Yes."

"So what does it matter, there's a ring? Just make the painting already."

Two days later, another phone call.

"Herman, the ring. It's showing through the gesso."

"Did you put the white lead down?"

"Not yet."

"White lead is impermeable. Don't worry."

The white lead covered the stain. Ron went to work on the painting. It wasn't until weeks later that the ring began to show through the paint, like the sun, like the headlight on a locomotive.

I knew enough to stay away from Ron during this period. In time, he appeared at my door, and asked to borrow my power saw. I could hear him using it upstairs, night after night, and imagined him cutting his creation into neat parcels, before consigning them to the Hudson River.

※ ※ ※

ONE of the displays at the American Museum of Natural History consists of some of Teddy Roosevelt's camping impedimenta. This includes an aluminum case fitted with lightweight editions of some forty or fifty of his favorite books, and various other ultralight or compact, or multipurpose gear he'd take with him into the wild.

You can learn a lot about a person from the possessions he chooses and how he takes care of them. T. R. was clearly a punctilious fellow, leaving nothing to chance— and he must have spent endless hours upstairs in the White House, going over his equipment. Making lists, weighing things, organizing and reorganizing gear for his next adventure.

Not unlike myself once upon a time. I did a fair amount of stomping along forest trails—and I was forever sending away in the mail for special Norwegian boot socks, and Geodetic Survey maps of New Jersey, or upgrading my hikers kit at Camp and Trail Outfitters in Manhattan.

This Camp and Trail Outfitters was on Chambers Street

in one of those old lofts dating from the middle of the nineteenth century. You had to have an idea where it was, or you'd never find it. The sign at the entrance was small, and lost among other similar signs. The flight of wooden steps leading to the place was long and steep, and there were travel posters of mountain scenes lining the narrow stairwell.

After making the ascent, one went through a door into a large room filled with the very fragrance of adventure. It was the period when lightweight rip-stop nylon and space-age plastics were just making their first appearance. Much of the gear with which the place was stocked was no different from that which made up the outfits of the early explorers—some of whom must have shopped there.

A bivouac tent made of wax-impregnated balloon cloth was set up in the middle of the room, Swiss- and German-made mountaineering boots, of specially tanned leather, stood on racks along the walls. Coils of silk rope, bunches of steel rings and spikes and gimmicks that mountain-climbers use hung from the rafters. There were zinc and aluminum mess kits and lanterns, and goose-down sleeping bags, and canvas rucksacks made on the premises.

Bustling around in the midst of all this were Mr. and Mrs. Simonow, the proprietors—an elderly couple. One assumed they'd met on an Alp.

Occasionally a burly guy would come in and tell Mr. Simonow that he wanted to outfit a party of eight for a spring assault on Mt. Passaic.

Simonow would go to a file cabinet and pull out a list.

"For Mt. Passaic, you'll need the following": then he'd read out the various exotic hardware, lengths and grade of rope, devices for comfort and shelter, and menus of dehydrated food.

If you bought boots from Simonow, he'd fit you with exquisite care, poking and prodding and feeling, shoving his finger down the counter while the boot was on your foot, an essential measurement. Then he'd send you charging up and down the stairway to see if the toes cramped while descending.

I have my boots yet. And my old Camp and Trails canvas knapsack, patched many times, the leather straps cracking, and my brass alcohol stove—no bigger than my fist.

I wouldn't know where to get stuff like that today. Suburban sporting goods stores began to have departments bright with nylon and aluminum camping gear from Japan and Korea, sealed in clear plastic. And after a while, Camp and Trail Outfitters closed its doors.

And the woods got crowded. In secret places where I had never encountered a human soul, I began meeting people carrying those bright backpacks.

I don't do anything that could be called hiking these days. There's a small National Historic Site not far from here, and I walk with my dog, Jacques, for an hour or so, every morning, on well-trodden paths. No need of a compass or waterproof matches.

Still there's the cold wind blowing off the river, and in the distance, I can see the blue Catskills. Today we watched a pair of eagles. It's a good compromise. And when I crave that fragrance of adventure, I can stick my nose into the downstairs closet.

※ ※ ※

I WAS good friends with a kid named Sean Flynn, in the fifth grade in military school. He was the son of Errol Flynn, the big actor. Sean was a neat kid. He was good at building model airplanes, and played flute in the junior band.

Sean was pulled out of school and taken east. Shortly after he'd left, I was sent to deliver a message to the band teacher, Captain Elkhart. I'd never been to the band room. But of course my friend Sean had spent a lot of time there.

Captain Elkhart was a friendly, white-haired type. "Well, young man, have you ever considered learning to play an instrument?" he asked me.

"I was thinking about taking up the flute," I said.

Captain Elkhart perked up. It was hard to get flute players. Not enough volume. There was a waiting list for loud instruments.

"Well, you know our flutist in the junior band has left school."

"I know."

"Take this note to your teacher. You can report here tomorrow at three, and we'll get you started."

The next day, Captain Elkhart showed me how to get a tone out of a flute—actually just the top joint of a flute, the part with the mouthpiece. It turned out you blew across the hole, like making a sound with a pop bottle, which I already knew how to do.

Then he drew a whole note, a half-note, and a quarter-note on a piece of paper towel, and explained what they were.

"Go in here, and practice," he said. He opened the door of a little closet. Inside were a chair, a light bulb, and a music stand. It was one of a row of closets. I went in. On both sides of me, other kids, in other closets, were honking and whistling and squeaking.

I spent time in the closet every school day. I progressed from blowing notes to scales, and finally simple tunes— and while I tooted, other, louder tooters were being tutored on both sides of me. I got so I could listen to what I was doing with a trombone blaring on my left and a trumpet on my right, each eighteen inches from my head on the other side of a thin piece of plywood.

I stayed with the flute through military school, and junior high, and high school—mainly because hanging around various band rooms was pleasurable compared to study hall, but my progress slowed from minimal to indiscernible. I was just good enough to play third flute in a section of three. If there had been four, I would have played fourth flute. But I always showed up for practice, and was good at carrying heavy stuff when the band went somewhere.

And I appreciated the music. I know the flute parts to all sorts of light classical and march music, such as high school bands play—lots of overtures, "Poet and Peasant," "Morning, Noon, and Night in Vienna," "Orpheus in the Underworld," and "King Cotton," "The Thunderer," and the dreaded "Stars and Stripes Forever," with the diabolical piccolo part.

But the knack of paying attention to something while distracting stuff was going on around me was the only thing I got out of my years as a flutist.

But, really, that's something. In college, I could study through dormitory riots and stampedes. I once comfortably wrote a book while the building next door was being demolished. And I can sleep on a bus carrying a large party of German tourists with a guitar *and* an accordion.

It's a handy thing to be able to do—but on one occasion it was more than that. I'm speaking of the time I first lived in Hoboken, when the ability to sustain concentration saved my sanity and probably my life—the time when I had to deal with the most hellish, most agonizing, most brutal . . .

In a very few pages you will know all.

☙ ☙ ☙

PEOPLE from the island of Puerto Rico are probably, on the average, a little nicer than people from most other places. They tend to be humorous, tolerant, and decent.

Puerto Ricans, I like you, but I hate your music. Also Cuban, Dominican—any music of the Spanish Caribbean. I have nightmares about it.

I didn't always have this prejudice. When I first came to Hoboken, I was prepared to rejoice in anybody's culture. But I changed.

Hoboken had a lot of bars. One side of River Street, across from the docks where the movie *On the Waterfront* was made, was nothing but saloons for four blocks. In later years, even the house where Marconi invented radio had a gin mill on the first floor.

A professor, who'd had a long career as a drunk, told me that when the bars in New York City used to close at 2:00 A.M. there would be a mass movement across the Hudson of those who were still athirst. In Hoboken the booze flowed around the clock. There was efficient ferry service, and if you started in lower Manhattan, it was just twenty minutes between drinks.

And further back, when the rest of the country had prohibition, Hoboken, for all practical purposes, didn't.

My loft in Hoboken was over a saloon. This was on Hudson Street, a block over from River, where only every other building had a bar in it. The establishment downstairs was known as the Taberna, and catered to the Hispanic community. The owner was a maternal type known as Mrs. Montana. I'd stop in for a beer or to use the phone when I was renovating my loft.

It was a cavernous place. The bar was at the front, and the rest of the huge room extended into darkness.

"Come in on a Friday or Saturday night," Mrs. Montana told me. "We have a band then."

"That's nice," I said.

I was not yet living in the loft. At the end of each day's painting and fixing, I'd cross back to Manhattan, where I was staying with a friend.

It was on a Friday that I finally brought over my last few

personal possessions and took up residence in the loft. I was puttering around, putting things away, when eight o'clock rolled around.

At first I thought it was an earthquake. A buzzing, grinding, rumbling under my feet. Then, for a moment, I thought some disaster in the harbor—tankers colliding, boilers exploding. After a time, I realized that what I was experiencing was sound. It was being generated from downstairs, from Mrs. Montana's saloon.

It was the band tuning up.

When they actually began to play, I had the sensation of the floor buckling and flipping. Like a trampoline. Like the cone of an enormous loudspeaker. I felt a painful popping in my ears, and my vision became blurry.

I remembered the cryptic remark of Herman Hermann, the art supplies dealer: "I know of a loft, but you have to like music."

The electric lights flickered rhythmically, crockery rattled on the shelves. Things like coffee mugs and ashtrays moved across tabletops. The glass in the windows visibly bent and pulsed in and out with each concussion.

And then . . . something that turned out to be an amplified human voice! This was most horrible.

I went down the stairs, holding on to both handrails, out into the street, and into the front door of the Taberna.

The far end, which had been dark when I'd come in during the day, was now illuminated dimly in red and blue. There were tables and chairs. Two or three people sitting, staring into their drinks, one couple dancing. At the very end of the room was a platform, four musicians— loudspeaker cabinets as big as automobiles were stacked on top of one another, and in the middle, surrounded by cables and huge ugly amplifiers, a guy yowling into a microphone held close to his mouth.

Not only was the band diabolically loud. They were lousy. They were inept. I learned later from Mrs. Montana that she didn't pay them anything—just let them play in her place out of charity.

"But they're horrible," I told her. "They only know six tunes. Surely they keep people away."

"It's slow around here on weekends, anyway," she told me. "People go to New York."

She felt sorry for the vocalist, the leader of the band. "He's a veteran," she said.

I was not going to give up the loft. And clearly, Mrs. Montana had the right to run her business any way she wanted. I had to live with the weekly concert.

I got so I could sort of tolerate it. Of course there were certain categories of things one couldn't do during the bombardment—like think. And friends who dropped by on a Saturday night tended to turn ashen and run out into the street after a while.

But I stuck it out, and the band stuck it out—right up to the time when the building—and all the other buildings, and all the bars, and Marconi's house—fell to the wrecking ball. Urban renewal. I was among the spectators when the old place went down. I thought it collapsed with a sort of Latin rhythm.

❧ ❧ ❧

I t's fairly certain that I'm not going to be appointed to high office, so there's no harm in my confessing my past use of narcotics. I have smoked marijuana—oh, five or six times. It was in the sixties and early seventies when everybody was doing it.

My most notable experience with mind-altering substances took place in Hoboken. Adjacent to my loft was a building known as the Casbah, where the hippies lived.

My back windows afforded a view of their back windows. The casbah was a five-story building with two apartments on each floor. In each apartment lived assorted freaks. They weren't first-rank hippies. Somehow they had failed to make it all the way to the East Village in New York, just a few miles to the east. They had put down roots in Hoboken, and there they did the best they could.

Ten south-facing kitchen windows I could see from my loft, and in each of them a mass of greenery. At night, special plant-encouraging lights created a bizarre electric/vegetable glow that lit up the tiny air-shaft-cum-backyard-cum-garbage-pit. These were the many pot plants that the inhabitants of the casbah tended.

The building was an urban farm. Seedlings were cultivated under the special lights, every window was crowded with cannabis fronds, and in summer, huge bushes in pots and barrels and ashcans waved in the breezes on the roof.

The hippies tended to dress in overalls and rubber boots. I could see them fussing over their crops with tiny scissors and watering cans. On the subway that connected with New York they would bring bags of plant food, peat moss, and fertilizer.

I enjoyed seeing all this industry. And I liked the sight of the marijuana bushes glowing in the night. A little touch of nature in the grim brick Hoboken scene.

And after a time, I conceived a wish to try their product. Easily done. When I ran into Luke, the leader of the commune, I asked him for a sample. Luke seemed flattered. Flushed with pleasure, he handed me a fat marijuana cigarette. I took it to my loft and made ready to have a psychedelic experience.

Knowing that the drug was supposed to enhance the enjoyment of music, I put on some appropriate sounds. The Dave Brubeck recording of *Die Fliegende Hollander*. I got comfy. I lit up.

This is what I experienced: Headache. Stomach cramps. Muscle pain. Profuse sweating. Deep depression. It lasted for six or eight hours.

I was later told that some strains of marijuana tend to make one feel good. Others tend to make one feel bad. This was evidently the feel-bad kind.

The next time I met Luke, I told him, "That reefer you gave me . . ."

"Yes?"

"It gave me symptoms worse than the flu."

"Yeh, it does that."

"You mean it makes you feel lousy every time you smoke it?"

"Terrible, man."

"But you and everybody in your building spend all your time tending and pruning and growing the stuff. Why do that if it makes you feel like garbage?"

"Hey, man! It's all we've got."

I've pondered that conversation for years. I still don't understand all the details, but the story covers a lot of situations I've encountered since.

❖ ❖ ❖

FOR the past twenty years or so, I have quietly observed the trend toward gussied-up eating. I have lived through Julia Child, Nouvelle Cuisine, Northern Chinese cooking, Perrier with a twist, mesquite barbecue, and all the food fads that have been thought up for us. Some I even like. I mean, pizza with broccoli is good. And you can eat around the broccoli.

But overall, my reaction to fashion food is this: ha! You may blacken all the redfish you like—I know there is nothing apt to be discovered or invented to surpass what I have experienced long years past.

I speak of the Original Spartacus A. P. Pepsi Cola Oriental Restaurant—the ultimate. It was known to regulars as the Original Spartacus—the sign outside displayed the full-length enigmatic handle. It was located on Twenty-fifth Street in New York, off Eighth Avenue, and it was as close to heaven as I expect to get.

It was a Greek restaurant. In the same sense that Praxiteles was a stonemason. Dim and dingy, lit by a few fluorescent fixtures, no one of them with more than one bulb working, it was frequented by artists, communists, and Puerto Rican cab drivers, some of whom were artists and communists.

The walls bore one of the last examples of the work of the Mad Muralist—a specialist in Levantine and Middle Eastern restaurants, whose hallmarks were stencils and silver radiator paint. In the case of the Original Spartacus, the motif was many silver Acropoles applied at various angles to the blue walls.

There was no menu as such. Jimmy, the proprietor, sized you up, and served you what he thought you needed. Some of Jimmy's creations were broiled porgies, dandelion salad, incredible tender lamb with orzo, coffee to raise the dead, and a sort of custard I've never encountered again.

The price for all this was determined by Jimmy's assessment of how much you appreciated his work. If you left anything on your plate, the price went up. If you ate every morsel (never a problem) the price went down, plus he'd toss in a salad or a few anchovies, or a glass of retsina. If there was a woman in your party, Jimmy would charge a dollar apiece, no matter what or how much you ate. If she was pretty, he'd contribute a free bottle of wine. And if she danced with him, no charge for the meal, and a bottle of wine for everyone at the table.

But it wasn't the quantity, the incredible cheapness, and the possibility that any meal at the Original Spartacus A. P. Pepsi Cola Oriental Restaurant might turn into a party . . .

What am I saying? Of course it was.

🌟 🌟 🌟

LOOKING back over my life so far, I am able to remember specific days that were perfect. These tend to be days, and parts of days, when nothing in particular happened, except that I was utterly happy. Summer days in country places make up a big part of the list.

I once visited Patti, a young woman I'd met in college, at her family's country house. Patti was a good painter, and good company. My girlfriend, Bertha, and I drove up with a big pail of steamer clams, and a couple of bottles of wine. The weather was perfect.

We sat under the trees, having eaten the clams, and drank the wine. We told stories, and looked at the sunlight on the fields, and gathered wild strawberries in the meadow beside the house. There were many easy silences during which we were aware of little breezes rustling the leaves.

Then, I saw a creature like nothing I'd ever seen before—something dark and furry and wild-eyed. It leaped straight up, above the tall grass, swiveled its head briskly from side to side, and dropped out of sight.

"Good lord! What was that?" I said.

"What was what?"

"Look! There it is again!" The creature had breached again, above the tops of the grass.

"That's just Charlemagne, our Maine Coon cat."

"Maine Coon cat? What's that?"

What it was, it turned out, when the animal got tired of

bounding through the grass—the leaps were its way of reconnoitering for game—and approached the veranda, was a cat with the dignity and aspect of a bull elephant, or a water buffalo. Its fur came down in greasy ringlets. It had tiny ears, and monstrous feet, little eyes that shone fire— and it stepped in such a way that one expected the ground to shake.

"That's the most formidable cat I've ever seen," I said.

"He sure is," said Patti. "Charlemagne is the boss of all the cats and dogs in the neighborhood."

"He's a Maine Coon cat, you say?"

"Maine Coon cat."

It was admirable. Also unapproachable. Only Patti could touch it. I was attracted to dangerous creatures in those days. I decided I'd own a cat like that some day.

Bertha moved into my loft in Hoboken. This is how it came about. I telephoned her at her apartment in Manhattan, and got a recorded message. The number had been changed, the message said. Then it said the new number. I wrote it down. It was familiar. "Whose number is this?" I asked myself. It was my number.

A little while later, Bertha walked in. "You had your number changed to my number," I said.

"That's right," she said.

"Why do that?"

"I live here."

"You do?"

"Yes."

"How long have you lived here?"

"Couple of weeks. You mean you didn't know?"

I was not as observant in those days as I later became. I hadn't connected anything with the fact that Bertha had already brought all her stuff over, and a couple of cats.

"Of course I did. Just kidding."

Bertha was studying painting, but she was shy and self-conscious. When she painted I was not permitted to look. The loft was one enormous room. I had to keep my back turned at all times when she was creating. Had I peeked, she would have had a violent fit with screaming and throwing dangerous objects. When she would go out, I would peek. The paintings were no good.

Bertha tended to hurl heavy or sharp-edged stuff at me when things were going wrong in her life, which was often. She was seeing a psychiatrist who had twin beds instead of a couch. They'd both stretch out. I suspected he wasn't actually qualified.

After a time, I came to wish that Bertha had not moved in with me. I sort of hated her. It came as a relief when she told me that she sort of hated me too. She loved her psychiatrist.

"I guess you'll be moving out," I said.

"Eventually. When I find a place."

❧ ❧ ❧

SHE didn't even look for a place. She had her job, and her relationship with her new boyfriend, who was also her psychiatrist. She said she didn't have time to look for an apartment.

"Besides," she said. "Ever since we admitted that we detest each other, we've gotten along quite well. Why can't I just stay here and be your roommate?"

"It's indecent. It's always been indecent. Why don't you move in with the psychiatrist?"

"What, and ruin everything? I learned my lesson. I'd stay here forever before I'd do that."

I had to get her out of there. But how? Confronting Bertha was dangerous. She was apt to fall back on violence right away. I had to think of a way to put pressure on her indirectly.

As far as I could tell, the only things in the world she actually loved were her two pet cats, Lugo and DePalma. If I could make my premises untenable for them, she might find someplace to take them.

"I'll be lonely when you finally move," I told her.

"Of course you will. Without me your life is nothing."

"Maybe I'll get a pet to keep me company."

"Better idea than putting another woman through hell."

My plan was a simple one. I'd get a wildcat or an ocelot somewhere. It would threaten to eat Lugo and DePalma, and Bertha would take them, and herself, elsewhere. I began making calls to wild-animal dealers.

I did locate a couple of sources for ocelots, but they turned out to be very costly, of delicate health in captivity, and potentially a little more dangerous than I needed. I wanted something domestic, but similar to a wildcat.

I remembered Charlemagne, the Maine Coon cat I'd seen at my friend Patti's house. A striking animal, something between a cat and a bulldozer. I'd always wanted one anyway.

It wasn't easy to find one. I made a number of calls to Maine, where, I was told, they were generally regarded as pests, and occasionally hunted for bounty. I hit pay dirt in the back room of one of those pet shops that used to exist around Chambers Street in lower Manhattan.

In a cage was a full-grown female the proprietors were keeping as breeding stock.

"She won't make a good pet," the pet shop guy said. "She's never been handled."

The animal was beautiful, long and rangy, yellow-eyed, and wild-looking.

"How much?"

"Twenty-five dollars."

The pet-shop guy put the cat in a sturdy box, and I took her home, across the Hudson, on the Hoboken Ferry.

Bertha wasn't around when I got home with the cat. I locked the two of us in the bathroom, and opened the box. She zipped under the bathtub, and peered out at me with those glowing, baleful eyes. I had provided myself with two pounds of hamburger and a book, *Moby Dick*—I thought it might interest her because it was about an animal. For the entire day, I read aloud to her, and offered her little balls of hamburger. It was hours before she'd accept one—another hour before she'd take a morsel from my fingers—and another hour before she'd suffer me to touch her. I decided to name her Zoe. From time to time, Lugo and DePalma, Bertha's cats, would sniff under the bathroom door. Zoe ignored them.

When Zoe and I had more or less made friends, I opened the door. Lugo and DePalma came right over to sniff the new visitor. One sniff was all it took.

Cats do not fight to determine the outcome. They know before they start who is going to be the winner. In this case there wasn't even a fight. Lugo and DePalma got one whiff of Zoe, interpreted what they had smelled, and vanished into thin air.

They intuited that Zoe was no climber, and took up permanent residence on the top shelf of the closet. Zoe, meanwhile, was strolling around the loft, treating it as her own—which, for all purposes, it now was.

Bertha came home, and discovered that she had to feed and tend her cats while standing on a ladder. When she tried to bring them down, they flew like birds back to the closet shelf.

Inside of a week, Bertha had found a suitable apartment, and moved her possessions, her cats, and herself into it— and Zoe and I settled down to a quiet life.

❦ ❦ ❦

My friend Magda invited me to come along and help her pick out a cat at Friends of Felines in Greenwich Village. It was a four story building, FULL of cats. The smell was astonishing.

The old lady in charge wandered around with a big stainless steel bowl ladling out blobs of ground-up hearts and gizzards, not paying much attention to us, as we inspected what seemed to be hundreds of cats.

On the second floor, I saw a Maine Coon cat, every bit as impressive as Charlemagne, the first Maine Coon cat I'd ever seen—actually the only one I'd ever seen other than my own coon cat, Zoe—and in her case, I'd taken it on faith that she was the genuine article. She didn't have the fierce unearthly look that first attracted me to Charlemagne. But this cat did.

"Look at this, Magda!" I said. "Take him! A Maine Coon cat!"

"I had a red cat in mind," Magda said.

"But look at this guy. He's terrific!"

Magda stubbornly refused to see the virtue of the bulky, ringleted, tiny-eared, big-footed, fiery-eyed beast. She found a marmalade cat in the last cage on the top floor, and went downstairs to fill out papers. The old lady dumped Magda's cat into a box, and I walked her to the subway.

Then I went back to Friends of Felines.

"That long-haired cat on the second floor," I said.

"Charlie? He's a Maine Coon cat, you know," the old lady said. "Want to take him home?"

I noticed that the old lady put on heavy leather and chain-mail gauntlets when she took Charlie out of his cage.

"How come the gloves?" I asked her.

"It's policy," she said. "Always use these."

"You didn't use them with Magda's cat."

"Just forgot, that's all," the old lady said. "Now, Charlie, you be a good boy—and don't come back!" she said to the cat.

I took Charlie home, and introduced him to Zoe. Without a moment's hesitation, he made to kill her. This was not a feint or a threatening display. It was a lunge. Zoe neatly got out of Charlie's way, by hopping up onto the windowsill.

Charlie appeared to lose interest in Zoe, and went around sniffing, acquainting himself with his new home. Zoe eyed him from the windowsill.

Suddenly, Charlie flew from the floor to the windowsill, and actually pushed Zoe hard enough to shatter the glass. What followed remains as a series of flashlight pictures in my mind. Zoe, astonished, passing through the smashing windowpane. Shards of glass in midair. Zoe vanishing. Charlie, methodically chipping away at Zoe's paws, which were desperately clinging to the edge of the outside sill, two stories above the street.

It seemed that less than a second had passed. I had stood frozen. Now I acted. I shouted. Charlie looked my way. This gave Zoe a chance to haul herself up onto the sill, and into the room. She dropped behind a radiator. In the same moment, I had picked up the nearest object and hurled it at Charlie. It was a plastic cottage-cheese container—one-pint size—full of royal purple ink. It whacked against the window frame, and burst open, drenching Charlie, who then hopped down and came straight for me. He wrapped himself around my foot, and sank teeth and claws through my sneaker.

When I shook him off, red blood was oozing through the white canvas. Now Charlie stood his ground, making a puddle of purple ink, waiting for my next move. He eyed me steadily. Zoe had the sense to stay behind her radiator.

My next move was to calm the cat down. I spoke to him. He seemed to soften a little. I approached and reached out a hand, tentatively. He raked it, leaving bloody stripes.

I began shouting for help, and my upstairs neighbor appeared.

This is what met his eyes. Me, faced off in the middle of the room with a soggy, shapeless, enraged creature. Blood and pools of purple something all over. The window, smashed.

"What the hell is it?" he asked.

"It's a cat."

He looked at the broken window. "How did it get in?"

"Just help me catch it."

It took maybe an hour until we were able to pounce on Charlie, and successfully shove him into his box. An hour after that, my wounds bandaged, I was in front of Friends of Felines. The old lady was still there. I could see her through the windows, moving around with her bowl of slop. I rapped on the door until she finally heard me and let me in.

"I brought him back," I said.

"I'm not surprised," she said. "That Charlie is such a bad boy. He always comes back."

She opened the box, and Charlie stepped out and rubbed his head against her, purring. The ink had dried, and he was a beautiful shade of purple. The old lady didn't seem to notice. She was cuddling him and saying, "Charlie, you bad boy. You always come back."

❦ ❦ ❦

HAVING Bertha for a roommate had a number of obvious advantages. One was that we could pool our grocery budgets and cooking skills. Bertha was able to make eggplant parmigiana. I was able to make a killer salad. Local jug wine was cheap (Villa Umbriago, bottled in Hoboken, was *incredibly* cheap), and decent fresh bread could be had at the bakery two blocks away.

The fact that we had exactly the same menu every night did not bother us. Bertha's eggplant parmigiana was excellent—and the salad had a lot of variety. Cost of components was minimal—and we were able to make enough for ourselves—and Herman Hermann, the art supplies dealer.

It so happened that our nightly meal coincided precisely with Herman Hermann's theories of health. He believed that it was vital to eat eggplant at least once a day. He himself was devoid of culinary skill, and had been known to eat eggplants raw, not knowing what else to do with them—but he got his daily quota.

So when Herman Hermann dropped in on us informally one night, he was delighted with the dishes we had prepared, and stayed until the last crumb, morsel, and drop were gone. When he appeared the next night and found we were eating the exact same meal, he was overjoyed and knew he had found kindred spirits.

Bertha and I liked having Herman Hermann for supper every night. We made a little family group, listening to Herman Hermann's stories until late at night.

Herman Hermann decided that Hoboken would be a perfect place to rent a cheap apartment to use as an etching ink factory. He had an ancient recipe for the stuff, and had already mixed up a batch. His customers loved it.

I've been told that in the old days, when etching was in flower, the old printmakers would go away out into the country to cook up their ink. Herman Hermann thought this was to preserve the secrecy of their formula—but I had been told it was to avoid the wrath of their neighbors. Apparently the fumes generated by the genuine good old stuff were intolerable at close range.

Herman Hermann contended that all that was needed

was a decent exhaust fan and a modern gas range. Notwithstanding, he had been evicted from the apartment building on Twenty-third Street where he had made his first ink—but not before the other tenants filed into the street, and two different fire companies plus the bomb squad had been called.

These details we did not exactly know when we advised Herman Hermann about available apartments in Hoboken.

He found a suitable place, just around the corner. It was old and primitive enough that all the tenants still heated and cooked with coal—which meant chimneys, a good updraft, the chimney pot on the roof, five stories above the street—with a decent breeze off the river no one would be able to identify the source of the . . .

. . . horrible, choking, eye-burning, sulfurous, frightening black cloud that soon became an irregular feature of the Hoboken night.

It didn't last very long. The other tenants found the monster out. They claimed their pets were dying. Herman Hermann said they were exaggerating—and besides, they were ingrates. From the time he had started making etching ink, not a cockroach had been seen in the building.

Herman Hermann dropped in for supper. "This may be the last time I can come for a while," he said. "I've found a place to make my ink in Amityville, on the Great South Bay."

It is ever thus. While complacent burghers lie abed, great men with burning ideas are stinking up the night.

❧ ❧ ❧

I AM fairly good at listening to the English of the foreign-born. I was raised, after all, by a father who, when speaking, was generally thought to be clearing his throat.

Not only can I make sense out of my native language when it is spoken with emphases in the wrong places, and vowels distorted unrecognizably—I can even mimic the accents of many speakers.

Except some. Most notably, except people from Viet Nam and other countries of that region. Of course, I am not talking about the likes of my colleague Duc Nguyen, whose English is better, and clearer, than mine, or anybody else's. I mean people more recently arrived. For some reason that musical, liquid accent of theirs—French mixed with Chinese—bewilders me completely. I am able to get one word out of twenty.

I remember an artist who hit New York about the same time I began my regular raids from Hoboken. A chubby, open-faced fellow, his name was . . . well, I never did quite know what his name was. We met at the Zen Institute. Both of us were toting portfolios—and we unzipped and compared drawings. His were very nice—and of course, I couldn't understand them.

Mine, he appeared to believe, were not only great, but were magnificent expositions of some Philosophy of Art, which he espoused, and of which his drawings too were examples. This is all guesswork, you understand, based on his expression, and the odd word at long intervals. His enthusiasm bordered on wild, and he hugged me many times before we parted company.

After that, I met the guy—let's call him Duck—wherever I went. I'd be prowling around the Village with my girlfriend, Bertha—and there he'd be, in the middle of a crowd of well-dressed, well-heeled-looking people. His face would light up. He'd flash a brilliant smile, and call to me, "Peeeenkawalawalawala! My specialawalawalawala flen!"

Duck would streak across the street, drape an arm around my shoulders, and tell me, rapid-fire, all sorts of confidences, news, tidbits about the people he was with—

not a shred of which would I understand—but I did have the impression that he was telling me about great good fortune, gallery shows, commissions, sales, grants. Then with much ardent hand-shaking and embracing, he'd be gone.

It was clear that he was doing a lot better than I was. I would pore over the lists of shows in New York, looking for a name that might be his. Whenever I'd see him his clothes would be a little more splendid, and the people with him more obviously bedrock rich.

The last time I saw him was in the men's room at the Museum of Modern Art.

Bertha had a useful father. He was a curator of the department of wallpaper and carpets in some museum out West. As a curator, he received invitations to all the black-tie openings at museums and galleries in New York. These he would forward to his daughter, who would share them with me.

By maintaining two barely passable costumes—for me a black suit, for her a second-hand dress of a kind that might be worn at such an occasion—we were able to augment our diet in considerable style. These museum openings had first-rate caterers, not to mention open bars. With Bertha's father's invitations, these evenings would be the cheapest of all dates. We'd look at whatever art was going, rub elbows with the rich and famous, and eat until we were bug-eyed, the idea being to take on enough nutrition to last a couple of days.

So there I'd be, sipping some wonderful liquor, and subtly trying to get into the background of a picture someone was taking of Robert Motherwell—and Duck would appear.

"Peeeenkawalawalawala!" And we'd be off—two cronies, chatting away like crazy. Exactly like crazy, because I would talk to Duck, pat his back and try my best to express the kind of happiness he was showing. There was no evidence that Duck was getting my drift any more than I was getting his.

The last time I saw him, in the men's room, he was wearing a cloth-of-gold sports jacket. That was the time he showed me his gold Museum of Modern Art card—the one that entitles the bearer to take the paintings home with him—and asked me if I'd been given one too.

After that—I never saw him again. I think he ascended to Nirvana. He showed up no more at Tuesday openings at the Modern or the Met.

In time, Bertha went her way, taking her tickets to the caviar and beef Stroganoff of the cultured rich. I sank back into the lower depths where I belonged. And Duck . . . Duck is somewhere, enjoying the rewards reserved for those who dispel the illusion of duality, and completely comprehend the nature of reality in the clear light of Buddha.

※ ※ ※

I USED to store my car in a garage down by the waterfront in Hoboken.

The one employee at the garage was an awkward-looking guy about thirty. Always wore a New York Yankees cap, and had a runny nose. He was known as "The Kid." I never heard him called anything else. He parked and unparked cars, and washed them. His boss, known as "The Gorilla," but not called that to his face, spent most of his time threatening The Kid, and hollering at him.

The Kid was a sad sack. I speculated, but didn't want to know for sure, whether The Gorilla and The Kid were father and son.

But The Kid, an object of abuse all day long, held a distinction shared by no other man in Hoboken.

He was the official master of Jolly Roger.

Jolly Roger was the leader of the dockside dog pack. There were maybe twenty-five of them—strays and feral dogs, and their offspring. They lived on the docks, were sometimes fed by the longshoremen, and scrounged a living in the alleys at night.

Jolly Roger had arrived on a ship from Alaska. He was part husky and part chow chow—blue tongue, bowed legs, curly tail. He weighed about fifty pounds, and had more dignity and authority than any dog I've ever known.

There was an iron fence that ran the length of River Street, the docks on the other side. Here Jolly Roger and his little band could be seen, safe from the dog warden. Often, I'd see him holding court. He'd be reclining, regally, on a little patch of grass, and each dog in turn would approach him, slinking, head held sideways, and crawl the last couple of feet to him, and rub its throat against his muzzle.

He'd allow the puppies to clamber over him and nap cuddled against his side.

I have seen Jolly Roger teaching another dog how to gather newspaper and build a nest under a parked car. I have seen him leading a raiding party up the alley behind Washington Street, overturning garbage cans, and carrying food back to the docks. And I have seen him, chased by the dog warden in his truck, run the wrong way up a one-way street, leaving the dog warden high and dry.

I never saw him in a fight. I did see him challenged by newcomers, and the newcomers subdued forever by one baleful look.

Jolly Roger would occasionally leave his pack and venture off by himself. I'd catch glimpses of him all over town, and as far away as Jersey City, Weehawken, and Union City. He was welcomed and known by name in all those places, and in all of them puppies resembling him were born.

Afternoons, one of the cooks from the Three-Star Chinese American Lunch would appear on River Street carrying a covered tray, head-high, waiter-style. A snack for Jolly Roger and one or two favored cronies.

Once, when the Hudson was mostly frozen, Jolly Roger ventured out to sit on the ice and meditate. The chunk of ice broke loose, and Jolly Roger floated out into New York Harbor. A passing Hoboken tug hailed him, he jumped off the ice, swam to the tug, and was hauled aboard. They brought him home, dignity intact.

Another time he was seen to fall into the river and drown alongside a freighter unloading in the slip. Three days later he appeared out of a storm sewer.

There was a period during which a suburban commuter who came to Hoboken in a Rolls Royce would take Jolly Roger home weekends. Of a Friday afternoon, he'd open the door of the Rolls, Jolly Roger would enter, and they'd spend the weekend on the estate in Saddle River. Monday, he'd bring Jolly Roger back. He had never been allowed to touch the dog.

And yet, once when I looked out the window of my second loft in Hoboken, down near the waterfront, I saw in the little cobblestone alley, Jolly Roger rolling on his back, waving his paws in the air, while The Kid tickled him and rubbed his belly.

I wonder how many people besides me envied that guy.

᭞ ᭞ ᭞

At one point Hoboken had a federally funded program for the purpose of enriching local culture. This could have been done satisfactorily by replacing all existing basketball hoops with new ones, but the staff of the program had bigger ideas. One day the administrator of the program called me on the phone.

"Mr. Pinkwater, you are a local artist."

"No—I'm an express."

"We were wondering whether you were acquainted with Alexander Calder."

"You mean do I know his work? I know it and admire it."

"But do you know him personally?"

"I shook his hand at the Museum of Modern Art once, but I don't think he caught my name."

"But you've met him. Perfect. I suppose you know that he went to school for a year right here in this town."

"Do tell."

"Perhaps you'd like to call him up and ask him if he'd spend a day with a bunch of first-graders here. They could cut things out of paper, and make mobiles."

"I'll bet you'd have a lot of pictures taken," I said.

"Oh yes, we'd make sure there was plenty of press coverage."

"I'm sure he'd be delighted," I said. "But tell me this, just in case he asks. Why should he agree to do such a thing?"

"Well, you could explain to him that it would be an opportunity for him to make a meaningful contribution to the cultural life of our community."

"Oh, good. I call him up and say, Mr. Calder, one of the greatest living artists—age oh, I don't know, maybe seventy-five. Drop what you're doing, put down your tin-snips or whatever, and come over to New Jersey so you can make a contribution to culture."

"Exactly. So you'll do it?"

"I wouldn't want you to entrust this mission to anyone else."

I don't have to tell you that Alexander Calder, as far as I was concerned anyway, was left to bend coathangers without interruption.

꽃 꽃 꽃

THERE were a number of colorful street characters in Hoboken, one of whom was Pancho Villa. Pancho Villa was a guy dressed in a Mexican-style cowboy suit, with a big sombrero. Spelled out in studs across the back of his suede jacket was "Pancho Villa."

Other times I saw him in something resembling an electric-blue policeman's uniform.

Mostly he would strut around, striking poses on street corners, throwing out his chest. Occasionally, he would do a little bit of hollering. He wasn't a specially outlandish street loony, just a character often in evidence.

One day I emerged from my loft, and discovered the public hallway completely dark. Someone had unscrewed the light bulbs from all the fixtures.

I stood in the darkness. I became aware of a presence—someone was sitting on the stairs a little below me—and a crunching noise. This person was sitting on the stairs eating nuts of some kind and tossing the shells around.

"Hey who's there?" I said.

No answer, just the crunching of nuts, and the tossing of shells.

"You'd better answer me," I said.

"It's Pancho Villa," the voice came back.

"Pancho, did you unscrew all the light bulbs, and are you now sitting on the steps eating nuts and throwing the shells around?"

"Yeh. So what?" Pancho Villa said.

"Well you've got no business here," I said. "I want you to begone."

"Don't make me laugh. I'm Pancho Villa."

"Look. You unscrewed all the light bulbs, and you're messing up the hallway. You don't belong here—so take off, all right?"

"Hey, don't get me mad. Do you know who you're talking to?"

"Yes. Pancho Villa. Now look, I'm not going to waste time with you. You clear out of here or I'm gonna call the cops."

"Ha. You call the cops. What does that mean to me? The cops can never catch Pancho Villa."

So I went back in the loft and phoned the police.

"Pancho Villa has unscrewed all the light bulbs in my hallway, and now he's sitting there eating nuts and tossing the shells around and he refuses to leave."

"We'll be right over," said the police.

Five minutes later they arrived.

We screwed the lightbulbs back in to the light fixtures. There were pistachio nut shells all over the hall. There was no sign of him.

"He was here a minute ago," I said.

"That's the way it always is," the police said. "We can never catch Pancho Villa."

🐝 🐝 🐝

NATIVE Hobokeners are less common than they used to be. Many of them were driven out of town by an influx of yuppie homesteaders. They were as warm and entertaining a bunch of people as people can be.

Da-salt-uh-da-eart is what they were, with some of the highest-grade eccentrics and loonies mixed in.

Also criminals. In my days in Hoboken, the two main topics of interest were politics and crime, which sometimes overlapped.

One of my acquaintances was Big Bob. Big Bob was said to be a persuader for a loan shark, and did other odd jobs that didn't bear thinking about. We had fatness in common, and we'd compare failed attempts to diet when we'd meet on Washington Street.

When Big Bob found out I was a writer, he became fired with the notion of being a confidential source.

"Eh, Pinky! You ought to go 'round wit' me faw a coupl'a days. You could write a whole book from what I do."

"Bob, I don't want to know what you do."

"That guy who wrote *The Godfather* musta never was in Joisey, or he woulda knew more."

"Bob, I don't write those kind of books."

"Yeh, butchoo could. I could tell you everything."

"Bob, I don't want to hurt your feelings, but you're a criminal. It wouldn't be healthy for me to know any details about your activities."

"Dat's the kinda prejudice I run into all the time, Pinky."

Big Bob met some policemen one night, as he was coming out of a warehouse with an armload of merchandise. For a few weeks he was out on bail, wandering around the streets, practicing his defense. "Ah'm innocent," he'd say. "Ah'm innocent."

When Big Bob came back from the state pen, he was down to about two hundred pounds, and had gone straight.

"I learnt a trade, Pinky," he said. "Leatherwoik. I stold the tools from da joint when I left. I make a pretty good buck at flea markets on da weekends. You want I should make yoo a belt wit a nood on it?"

One day, having since moved to the country, I'd

managed to make it to Hoboken for a bucket of steamers at the Clam Broth House. Who should be sitting there but Big Bob? He was sucking up linguine. He'd gotten fat again.

"Ey, Pinky!"

We had a nice chat. The Iran-Contra hearings were going on at that time, and Big Bob had been following Oliver North's testimony.

"I don't get it," Big Bob said. "How come he doesn't want ta go to jail? He was s'posed to be da fall guy, right? Well da fall guy goes to jail. Instead, dis guy starts in to mention people.

"G. Gordon Liddy went to jail. He never spilled a single woid. I don' want to say anythin' against a Lootenant Coinel in the Marines—but dis guy strikes me as very unprofessional."

IF you're of the opinion that I'm just a zany who talks about inconsequential things, listen up. This is serious. This is about something profound—maybe spiritual. I'm talking about free lunch.

When I first struck Hoboken in the mid-nineteen-sixties, the institution was still alive, and I'm a better man for having experienced it.

The famous Clam Broth House in Hoboken. In the period I'm telling about, there was a restaurant, and an adjacent bar. The bar was not open to women. Men only. I'm just reporting—no inferences should be drawn.

The place was always crowded. On the floor was sawdust. People tossed their clamshells on the floor, and when you walked, you crunched.

You could order a beer, or a shot, or a shot and a beer. A

bucket of steamer clams cost something negligible, like a dollar and a quarter. That was for a *bucket*. A pot of steamers, which was smaller, was available for less.

For the landlocked I'd better say something about steamer clams, also known as soft clams, steamboat clams, elephant clams. They're dark grayish and small, with a bizarre tubular appendage looking a little like an elephant's trunk sticking out. These are not the clams you eat raw with a squirt of lemon a half-dozen at a time. They're steamed in a great double boiler, with perforations in the bottom of the top part. The bottom of the boiler, which has a faucet on the side, comes to contain clam broth, a distillate of clam juice, which the gods drank on Olympus.

When you come to eat steamers, you grab the little trunk, and remove the clam—toss the shell on the floor—and holding the trunk, you swish the clam end in a cup of clam broth, getting rid of the sand. The effete may then dip it in drawn butter, but that only slows you down. Some bite off the trunk, some eat it. Most remove the wrinkly sheath from the trunk if they do eat it—but these are unimportant distinctions of style. What matters is they are among the most delicious things on earth.

One paid for clams, and also for fresh-sliced corned-beef and pastrami sandwiches that took both hands to deal with—but the clam broth was free. Also, scrag-ends and splinters and shards of corned beef, slices of bread, baked beans, onions—you get the picture?

For the price of a beer, a man could assemble a small feast. And the company was choice. Dockers and tugboat men, guys in reefer jackets and yellow foul-weather gear. The room was low-ceilinged and smoky, and all the woodwork was black with age. Genuine swinging doors, of course. You stepped through those and went straight back a hundred years.

Charles Dickens could have done this justice. He lived in Hoboken for a while, and must have dropped in here, or to a similar establishment, to pump up his vitamins and cock an ear to the local dialect.

This is not to be construed as an advertisement for the Clam Broth House. It's been years since I last ate there, and I have no idea of its present condition or mode of operation. Lately, I was told that they're contemplating installing a dinner theater, but I choose to ignore malicious gossip like that—probably shouldn't have mentioned it.

꽃 꽃 꽃

BOXED in by the back ends of three Hoboken tenements, including mine, was an open space perhaps thirty feet square. The two windows at the end of my loft overlooked it. On the fourth side, where there was no building, there was a high wooden fence.

It was a backyard belonging to a building known as the Casbah, around the corner on Second Street, where a variety of hippies, freaks, and young people lived rough and paid no rent. It was the sixties. There was no access to the yard from my building or the semiderelict apartment house opposite.

Cats would come over the fence, and sometimes kids, who would stomp around on the immense pile of garbage that filled the space.

The debris was at least a fathom deep when I first moved there. It got progressively deeper. At night, sounds would come from the space between the buildings—the rumble of a window sash being lifted, followed by the crash of a full bag of trash hitting the heap, followed by the sash being shut.

It was my fellow citizens across the way who were in the habit of airmailing household waste, thus saving the bother of a trip down to the row of ashcans at street level.

At times, this sequence would be followed by the sounds of other windows being opened, occasionally mine, and imprecations shouted into the darkness. ''Y'ghaddam pig!''

Months and years rolled by, the swales and mounds became more monumental. And one kept one's windows at that end shut tight in the summertime.

There came to live in the Casbah a studious-looking and taciturn young man, Mark Molloy by name. One afternoon in spring, I heard him exhorting some of the local kids down in the garbage pit.

''So if you'll help me clean all this up, you guys'll have a neat place to play. What do you say?''

Mark provided a wheelbarrow, and some shovels and rakes. He and a gang of kids worked at the gigantic compost heap for weeks. They bagged and dragged the refuse out to the street, where the Sanitation Department picked it up incrementally. In the beginning, it didn't look as though they were making a dent—then it began to appear that there was slightly less garbage. One day, actual earth became visible in a corner.

All through the days of the cleanup, passive, their elbows on the windowsills, my neighbors watched their accumulated leavings and sweepings being carted away.

In time, the tiny square was waste-free, raked. Grass seed scattered. A little path that went nowhere, bordered with stones. A couple of salvaged chairs. The kids were proud and delighted—but after a week or so of bringing their friends to show off their handiwork, they began to fade away. These Hoboken kids had no idea of what one did with a backyard, and truth to tell, neither did Mark. I saw him sitting in one of the chairs once or twice, reading a book—but he didn't appear to be all that comfortable.

Then toward the fall of the year, I remember hearing for the first time—again—the old sequence. Rumble— whiz—crash. When the snow began to fall, once more there was a growing mosaic of plastic bags from Shop-Rite, and the antique practice of fouling the nest went on as it had since men first gathered to live together.

※ ※ ※

A COUPLE of winters ago I was in New York City around Christmastime, showing a friend some of my favorite sights. This meant I got to take my first ride in years on the Staten Island Ferry.

We got to see the guy who rode the ferry for a number of years selling goods to the passengers. He had an assortment of cold-weather gear.

"You need this muff, 'cause the hawk don't bluff," he said. "Buy a scarf so you won't freeze, sneeze, or catch a disease. Step up and place your order, it's Macy's on the water."

I thought he added something to the ride.

There were some itinerant musicians on board, performing for donations tossed into the open guitar case. One of them did a nice medley of Caribbean numbers as we pulled into the slip in Staten Island—temperature twenty degrees. Made us feel like we were on a cruise.

On the way back, the guitar player was joined by his partner—a flamenco dancer. This guy was good. He had the little jacket, the pants, the shoes—and all the moves. Smiled all the time, too. He was maybe thirty, thirty-five pounds too heavy for that kind of work, but he put his heart into it. I dropped a couple of bucks for a fellow artist.

I was always over the maximum for that sort of activity, but I did enjoy a certain reputation at one time. I owned a black cashmere overcoat in which I looked pretty good—next to brand-new, and a perfect fit—and a friend brought me a present from a vacation in Spain—one of those flat round broad-brimmed hats, like the one on the guy on the sherry bottle. Rudolph Valentino is often pictured in one with little pom-poms around the brim. Mine was less frivolous, more formal, no pom-poms. I cut quite a figure around the artistic district in Chicago, which was home to a fair number of Hispanic types. Once, making my way along Welles Street, I overheard someone say, "Hey, here comes that fat flamenco dancer." I was also known in the neighborhood as "the fat bullfighter."

Another illustration of the adages "Handsome is as handsome does," and "Clothes make the man."

※ ※ ※

In the late sixties, a friend of mine who owned a handsome brownstone in the Village was drinking in a bar. There he became acquainted with a couple of Irishmen who specialized in executing big paintings on the sides of buildings. This was during a brief period during which many property owners in New York were muralizing blank walls in the interest of making their buildings look snappy. The cartoon for the wall painting would be divided into numbered squares, and up the two Irishmen would go, on their scaffold, charts in hand, and paint you anything you liked.

My friend struck a deal with the two mural guys. For a price, a design of my friend's choosing would be executed on the side of his house, facing Eighth Avenue. He came to me with the proposition.

"What sort of a mural would you like?" I asked him.

"You're the artist. Design something you feel is right."

"I don't have to go up on the scaffold, right?"

"Right."

I agreed to design the wall painting, and said I needed some time to think it over.

This conversation took place during a period in my life when my psychotherapy was starting to pay off. Instead of roistering around the streets like an antisocial beatnik, I tended to carry a briefcase and wear sport jackets (with hand-woven neckties in ghastly colors, not to lose identification with the Arts). My friends included psychologists, urban planners, and optometrists—young professionals. I too was a young professional. I was taking an intensive course in art therapy, and working as an art teacher in a number of settlement houses around New York. Every Friday I would attend a seminar uptown. There I would look at and discuss color slides of pictures painted by disturbed kids on the East Side—and I would show and discuss color slides of pictures painted by disturbed kids on the West Side.

I had located a number of cheap and exotic hole-in-the-wall restaurants, and I would take female youth workers to these, and to off-beat recitals, plays, and concerts— tickets to which were free—this suavity in contrast with my former dating style of inviting women to fall by my place for pizza and/or sex.

Of course all this folderol was merely a means of creating a fallback position should my efforts in the Art World come to naught—a possibility which more resembled a likelihood every day.

The actual job—the part where I dealt with kids of various ages in various settlement-house art rooms— always at the top of five flights of stairs or in a basement with maybe one window—was interesting, to say the least. I was fascinated by the intentness with which the kids addressed their work—and I was impressed at how successful they were at conveying what they wanted to convey. I don't flatter myself that my teaching inspired them. My program was to take away confining adult influences, and as soon as the kids caught on, I became superfluous.

I became a voracious observer. I was getting a handle on how these kid-artists were seeing things, learning what part of their expression was individual and what part of a kid-art-language. I took to carrying a camera in my brief-case, and after the kids had gone, I'd photograph their paintings in order to organize and study the slides later.

And while all this was going on, I was a frequent guest at the home of a couple who were my most enthusiastic collectors. They were my only collectors. They owned four large prints and a sculpture which were the work of my hand.

This couple, the Silvers, had in me a genuine artist who was guaranteed to show up at any party they might throw, and stand around, looking fierce, beside samples of his own work. In them, I had hosts who would unfailingly invite me to parties where I could stand around, looking fierce, beside bought-and-paid-for examples of my own work.

My subsidiary function at the Silvers' parties was an element in matchmaking. At each party there would be an unmarried female friend, and she and I would have been notified in advance to check one another out. On one occasion, I got hold of the wrong woman, and found myself in conversation with an editor of children's books. It was suggested that I might try my hand at illustrating. I was all for it—and a couple of weeks later, having written a text in order to have something to illustrate, I had a contract with a big publishing house in New York. Work-ing on the drawings—and even more, the writing—was intensely pleasurable. What was more, they had paid me money and promised more. This was truly an enjoyable diversion.

And more yet was happening! After years of my wish-ing, hoping, and trying, the great curator Una Johnson had selected a print of mine for inclusion in the Brooklyn

Museum Biennial—the Kentucky Derby for printmakers. Prior to this, I had made the rounds of every gallery in New York, and had been told in a variety of styles to get lost. Una Johnson had been the only one to see anything in my work, and now she had picked a great big woodcut, three by three feet, to hang in this prestigious exhibit.

Naturally, I was at the by-invitation-only opening, hobnobbing with the big artists. My date was a book editor. I was starting to move in literary circles. There was my print, hanging between a Jasper Johns and a Carol Summers. I was in there with the real guys!

The next day, when the exhibit was open to the public, I was there, strolling, looking, eavesdropping. I was mad to find out what the reaction of complete strangers would be to my work of Art. Most people just passed by. One or two lingered for a moment, leaned forward to read the name of the artist off the card. The next day, I caught a couple discussing it. The woman leaned back and pointed one toe upward. The man stroked his chin.

"Mystical," he said. Then they moved on. They'd spent maybe fifteen seconds in front of my picture. They hardly had time to focus.

The third day I began to get mad. "Who are these bozos?" I wanted to know. "What's the point been of my living cheap and spending all my money on art supplies? The kids in my classes pay better attention to what they're looking at than these museum cooties. Much better."

Something was happening to me. I'd spent four solid years trying to get something started as an artist in the Big City, and now it was starting to start—and I wasn't liking it.

And I realized that the whole time that I'd been trying to figure out what sort of mural to design for my friend's wall, I'd been thinking of it in terms of what somebody maybe eight years old would see on his way to school. I'd identified my audience.

HIGH NOON
AT THE
TYPEWRITER

My early years at the Louis B. Nettlehorst Elementary School on the north side of Chicago did not have any high points. Like everybody else, I trudged to school, sat at a little desk in a large unadorned classroom, and was taught by teachers who didn't appear to want to be there any more than I did. I was taught the rudiments of reading and arithmetic. I got to practice writing. About once a month the kids were marched to the auditorium to see films. *The Story of Tapioca* is one I remember.

When my class was taken to the public library—I guess it was in second grade—there was no kindly specialist librarian to cultivate my interest in books. The lady there told us the rules, said if we broke 'em she'd throw us out, and issued us cards.

That was good enough for me. I'd already been having my interest in books cultivated for a number of years.

There were ongoing games in the connected backyards of my block. These games were reenactments of historical events and books. In addition to Bull Run, San Juan Hill, and the battle of the Marne, some of the games we played included The Three Musketeers, Mysterious Island, and the Hunchback of Notre Dame. Nemo and Quasimodo were the roles you wanted to play. We were only dimly aware that our games were based on books. The battles, I now surmise, had been acted out in those very backyards since the time of the wars they had taken place in. I don't recall any portrayals of World War Two battles, although that war was going on at the time. Too current. The next generation of kids would select events from that conflict from the vantage point of history.

The books we played had been read by our older brothers and sisters, who told us the stories, and even supervised our enactments. An eleven-year-old might stand to the side, like a movie director and organize the imaginary jousting from *Ivanhoe*.

This was Chicago, not Cambridge, Massachusetts. I am not describing some elite bunch of kids, children of college professors. For the most part, we didn't even come from particularly bookish households. Reading was simply a legitimate kids' entertainment, like movies, and comics.

I myself learned to read from comic books. I can remember the actual moment when I became able to "code-bust," as they say. As a second-semester first-grader, I purchased a Batman comic—the first brand-new comic I ever owned. I had invested a dime. It was my own property. I was going to read every word in the thing or be damned.

And I did. I figured it out. I pored over it. I remember Batman was telling Robin about how they were able to scale some building because of their athletic prowess.

Scale? Athletic prowess? I knew those words weren't in the first-grade reader. But I had gotten through them! I knew what Batman and Robin were talking about! "Hey! I can read this! I can read anything!"

And I could. And I did.

Most of what I've done for the past twenty years is write books for kids. Much as I love doing it, careful and conscientious as I may be about it, I can never provide raw material that will motivate like that—simply because a kid cannot buy a book of mine for a coin, roll it up and shove it in his back pocket, and read it in some private place, without an adult in the world knowing what he's up to.

❧ ❧ ❧

THERE was this kid in my junior high school. Like me, he was a transfer student from back East. The school was in Los Angeles. The kid's name was Arnold Marmelstein. He dressed and acted a little differently from the rest of us. There was nothing outstandingly weird about him—just a few variations in style. For example, he wore those black-and-white saddle shoes, which we'd seen in Archie comics, but never on a living person. He was marked as being oddly different by kids who were in classes with him, and more or less ignored by everyone else.

In this school, they used to turn us loose in a big open court, with benches and trees. We'd eat our lunch out there. Mornings, before school, you could go there, and for a few cents, buy things like danishes and hot chocolate. They also had a break at midmorning, known as "Nutrition," during which you could get more danishes, and also tuna fish and peanut butter sandwiches. In the afternoon, they'd let us out again, and sell us candy bars, popcorn, and other snacks.

The native California kids all got tall. I just got fat—but that's another topic. What I mean to say is that the entire student body spent a considerable part of each day wandering around that lunch court, noshing and talking.

One day, Marmelstein strolled around the lunch court before school, addressing everyone he met. "I'm a Martian, did you know that?"

When Nutrition time came around, he continued to do it. "Did I ever mention that I'm a Martian? Yep, I come from Mars. My mother and father are from Mars. My grandparents still live on Mars."

At lunch, and at the afternoon popcorn break, he kept it up. By the end of the day, there couldn't have been a kid in the school who hadn't been told, by Marmelstein, twice, that he was an extraterrestrial, notwithstanding that most of them had no idea who he was, and had never spoken with him before.

I found his behavior puzzling. It wasn't much of a joke, if that's what he intended it to be—and he had worked at it all day long. Kids walking home from school talked about nothing but Marmelstein's statement of planetary origin.

The next morning. Outside the school. Two kids meet. The first one asks, "Do you believe he's a Martian?"

"No," the second kid says, and the first kid bashes him in the nose.

Elsewhere on the school grounds, another kid asks yet another kid, "Do you believe?"

"Yes," says the kid, and gets bashed in the nose.

A number of fights broke out during morning Nutrition. Two or three noses were bloodied, and someone had his glasses broken.

By lunchtime, people were throwing punches everywhere. Some kids hit only those who said they believed. Some kids hit those who said they did not. Some kids would hit you no matter what you said. And after a while, some kids would just make a preemptive attack on anyone who approached them.

Phil Wilson, the smallest kid in my gym class, jumped up on the shoulders of Tod Spaulding, the biggest kid in my gym class, and knocked him out cold.

Roger Arnoff went crazy, and flailing like a windmill, waded into groups of kids, and struck out at believers and nonbelievers alike.

Jane Romero pulled the hair of Jane Kirschner, her best friend, who was an unbeliever, and also kicked her.

I, personally, struck a number of unbelievers smaller than myself.

Arnold Marmelstein was nowhere to be seen. He had stayed home from school that day.

Before it was over, the police were called. The school was ringed with squad cars. Officers with bull horns dispersed us, and cautioned us to walk away from the school in groups of two and three. Motorcycle cops cruised slowly up and down the streets around the school, eyeing us.

The next day, a heavy police presence still in evidence, Arnold Marmelstein was sent for by the principal.

"You caused a riot," the principal said.

"What did I do?" Marmelstein asked.

"You said you were a Martian."

"And by doing that I caused a riot?"

"Yes."

"I told a story, that's all."

It's hard to believe that people could get so worked up about a simple fiction. But these things happen.

₩ ₩ ₩

A FEW years ago I saw a movie on TV about the life of Gustav Mahler. It was a stinker, more or less, except for the beginning. The beginning was great. I really enjoyed it. I also recognized it as a short story by Isaac Babel called "The Awakening." The film-maker had lifted the story, without crediting the author, intact and almost verbatim. Babel, like a lot of Russians, had disappeared in the late 1930s—so presumably the thinking was "Who's gonna sue?"

The reason I mention it now is that a curious insight arises from the only change in the text (aside from renaming the central character Gustav Mahler).

In the original story, a kid is signed up for violin lessons in old Odessa. His family hopes he'll turn out to be a prodigy and get them clear of poverty and disaster. The kid has no aptitude or interest, and commences to skip his lessons and hang around the harbor with some other boys.

There's an old man, a sort of ad hoc youth worker and swim coach. He takes pity on Babel's character, who has no aptitude for swimming either. The old man asks the kid what he wants to be when he grows up. The kid says he wants to be a writer.

"OK," the old guy says. "So what kind of tree is that?"

The kid doesn't know.

"You want to be a writer, and you don't even know the names of trees?" the old guy asks. "How can you be a writer when you don't know the names of trees?"

This impresses the kid. Later, his family finds out he's been skipping lessons, and there is a poignant scene in which the father pounds on the door of the bathroom into which the kid has locked himself, and the kid experiences terror, despair, and a sense of dedication to . . . learning the names of trees. It's very good in the film.

The change I referred to comes in the scene with the old swim coach. In the movie, the old man asks little Gustav Mahler what he wants to be when he grows up, and little Gustav tells him he wants to be a composer of music. (Don't even worry about why such a kid would be cutting his violin lessons—there's even better illogic.) The old guy says, "A composer, huh? OK, so what kind of tree is that?"

Young Gustav Mahler doesn't know.

The old guy says, "You want to be a composer and you don't even know the names of trees? How can you be a composer when you don't know the names of trees?"

The thing that strikes me, years after seeing the movie, and decades after reading the story, is that the premise is ridiculous in both cases. What has knowing the names of trees got to do with anything? And yet, for years I suffered from a sort of complex arising from ignorance of the nomenclature of woody plants.

It's not that I haven't tried—and I do know a number of tree names—it's just that I can't associate those names with actual . . . things . . . growing in the forest. I guess I'm well-enough educated in other respects, a graduate of extensive psychotherapy, and a terribly bright guy to begin with. Even so, for long years I was utterly paralyzed and did not begin my career as a writer of fiction—entirely because of deficiencies in woodlore. It may well be that when I did get started writing I chose to inhabit the ignominious swamp of children's literature because I knew I was just not good enough to write *real* books about human relations and sex—not good enough because I don't know my ash from my elm.

I am not the only one to have been afflicted with this belief that the naming of trees is a prerequisite to literature. Obviously, Babel was concerned with the idea—and Vladimir Nabokov reportedly registered shock when one of his students at Cornell couldn't name the trees in the quad.

Where does this notion come from? Could it have its origins in some druidic tradition? Why should I know about trees? I've lived most of my life where there hardly were any. And these days, living surrounded with them, why can't I admire them without getting intimate? Live and let live, I say. I don't bother them, and they don't bother me. Same as with snakes.

I want to point out that in his story, Babel himself mentions only two kinds of trees, acacias and lilacs (which I looked up, and they are more properly a shrub). It doesn't hurt the story. He gets by fine with just acacias. I submit that an author could write a lot of short stories, or a lot of novels, and mention no other trees than acacias with excellent effect.

I myself have written a ton of stuff without specifying trees—and no complaints. Oh, I get complaints—I hear from religious lunatics accusing me of being a devil worshipper, and chiropractors complaining that I don't show their profession sufficient respect—but I am never criticized for being inexplicit about flora of any kind.

I wonder how many other writers and aspiring writers are intimidated by their own lack of familiarity with leaf shapes, bark textures, and characteristic outlines.

Down with this pointless and probably antique preoc-
cupation with tree names! It should be extirpated root
and branch!

※ ※ ※

TODAY, some remarks about genius from one who
should know. As I see it there are two basic forms of
creative genius—one in which the gifted person makes an
important contribution, as in the case of Mozart, and the
other in which the genius simply has an unusual number
of quirks often to no purpose, which would tend to describe me.

(Although I often wish I had lived at the same time as
Mozart. I could have been of considerable help to him. We
might have worked on a comic strip together.)

The dictionary defines genius as applied to what I'm
talking about as: *an extraordinary intellectual power especially
as manifested in creative activity.*

I have that. Maybe not all the time—but half the time,
which makes me, I guess, a half-genius. Some would say
half wit.

Continuing with Mozart as an example, he was observed to be able to sit down and knock out music with no
apparent effort. It may be that Mozart simply *saw* this
music completely finished, and then merely copied it
down—as he himself claimed—or it may be that the pro-
cess of composing, trial and error, working things out, was
the same in his case as in that of any normal composer—
only much much faster—so much so as to be impercepti-
ble, maybe even to himself.

I suspect the latter. On a few occasions I have caught a
fleeting glimpse of my own creative machinery at work.
There appears to be a portion of my subconscious dedicated

to fooling with syntax, grammar, and style. When I have accidentally snuck up on this obscure area of mental activity, writing and rewriting phrases, sentences, and paragraphs is going on at a shocking rate.

I'm not talking about me consciously working at writing something. The function I describe just goes on by itself, playing with some random sequence of words, lengthening and shortening, swapping elements, changing emphasis, trying out one way and then another—endlessly, all the time. I've caught myself at it at odd moments, often when tired, or while doing some repetitive task.

It may be as a result of this endless involuntary writing lesson that I become a sort of lightning editor and reviser. I'm one of those guys who can write a page of prose while talking on the phone. And it's probably the reason I'm so intolerant of editors, whose whole job is to do something—usually badly—which comes to me as naturally as peristalsis.

I think I developed this tic, this habit of constantly experimenting with word order, and nuance of meaning, as a kid in grade school. I remember loving the grammar and logic exercises—the ones that went "Tapioca is to an iron foundry as (choose one) (a.) fish bait is to the houses of Congress, (b.) an avocado is to Frank Sinatra, or (c.) amoxycillin is to the National League." Loved those.

I read somewhere that Hindu holy men will repeat prayers until, whatever else they're saying or doing, the prayers go on within them constantly, waking and sleeping.

It may be something similar with my internal editorial department. And it may have been that that early compulsion to practice all the time is what made Mozart and me what we are today.

※ ※ ※

FRIENDS, it's my sad duty to announce that our civilization is doomed. I've known this for a couple of weeks now—but I didn't have the heart to tell you.

Somehow, without our realizing it, we have become a nation of the humor-impaired.

Have you noticed how often people say a thing is weird, when they ought to say it's funny. As in "I saw this movie. It was weird."

"You mean with a mad scientist, and the living dead, and bats, and like that?"

"No. Not scary. It was . . . weird. Y'know, full of jokes and stuff."

People who are funny are considered weird. The implication is that if one says things that evoke laughter one is crazy, and perhaps dangerous—an atavistic flashback to the days when one of our ancestors would get hold of some bad reindeer meat and go nuts, rolling around the cave, gnawing rocks, while the other hominids laughed nervously.

People have taken to apologizing for me when they introduce me. "This is Pinkwater. Don't mind him, he's a little weird."

A friend of mine tells me that in Los Angeles, when you say something funny, people say, "That's funny." Just like that. No laughter. "That's funny."

I don't know how this state of grimness came about. It appears to be some ghastly aftermath of the yuppie era. The implications are obvious—and dire.

A nation that holds humor at arm's length is in deep trouble. And we used to have such a robust sense of humor—now more and more people appear to be uncomfortable with the comical. . . . It's . . . it's weird.

HOW to tell if you are humor-impaired.

I've devised a simple test. First I spring a joke on you without warning:

What does a dyslexic, agnostic insomniac do?

[short pause]

He sits up all night wondering if there is a dog.

[longer pause]

If you laughed, chuckled, smiled, or smirked, your score is 3.

Did you groan or moan? If so, your score is 2.

Did you say or think the word "weird"? If so, your score is 1.

Are you still waiting for the joke? Score zero.

If you scored 3, your sense of humor is intact.

If you scored 2, there may be some degree of impairment, or you've already heard the joke.

If your score was less than 2, you are humor-impaired.

If you scored less than 2 and are an attorney, submit your application for employment to the Legal Department, National Public Radio, Washington, DC.

THIS is another bulletin on dealing with the humor-impaired. Our country is not the only one to be blighted by widespread humor loss—and not the first.

Today's example is a joke as told by almost any European, and especially my father or any of his friends.

"I'll tell you a joke. It's funny. You'll laugh.

"Here's the joke. So this guy is looking. Looking on the ground. Looking for something. Under a streetlight he's looking. Wait, this isn't the funny part yet.

"So here comes another guy, and he's helping him look. He's looking . . . the first guy is looking. They're looking. Oh! I forgot. The first guy lost his keys. It's his keys he's looking for.

"OK. This gets funny soon. So the second guy finally says, 'I can't seem to find them. Are you sure this is where you lost them?'

"Wait a minute, you're almost going to laugh now. It's almost. And the second guy says, 'No, I lost them over there.' Don't laugh yet.

"In a second comes the funny part. The second guy says, 'If you lost them over there, why are you looking for them here?'

"OK, get ready to laugh. The first guy says, 'The light is better over here.' OK, now you laugh."

It's a doomed world.

🐛 🐛 🐛

SOME of my friends have accused me of selling out. This is because of my writing things they regard as worthless commercial junk.

I am cut to the quick by these imputations. I have always produced lots of worthless junk—just it wasn't commercial. Now and then, when I get the chance to earn a few dollars, do I have to listen to people who want to be my aesthetic conscience? Fooey.

This takes me back to my days as an apprentice beatnik

in Chicago. One of my most beloved haunts was an establishment known as Maxie's Bookstore. Maxie's was not far from Newberry Park, also known as Bughouse Square. Chicago's speaker's corner, where anybody at all could harangue an audience on any topic for as long as they could hold their attention.

In the cold weather, the Bughouse Square regulars migrated indoors to Maxie's.

It was open all night, and usually crowded with insomniacs, hoboes, political radicals, artists, poets, zealots of various kinds, and chess bums. In the back of the store was a table set up with chess boards.

One of the regular chess players was a favorite of mine. He parted his greased-down hair in the middle, and always wore his jacket buttoned up to the neck. In a tight game, he would unbutton his jacket to reveal one of what appeared to be a numberless collection of lurid hand-painted neckties. Lurid is too weak a word. Ghastly they were. They had the effect of badly distracting an opponent, and giving the edge to the guy with the hair.

Another character who came in all the time was the Tiger's Milk man. Tiger's Milk is now a commercial product, available at health-food stores in powder form, as cookies, candy bars, and for all I know, furniture polish. Then, you had to make it yourself. The Tiger's Milk man was forever reciting the formula, which included brewer's yeast, blackstrap molasses, wheat germ, and I forget what else. He claimed it had restored him to obnoxious good health from a walking wreck. He'd whip off his hat and point to an almost bald head and say "See that? New growth! Tiger's Milk."

There was an Indian yogi who'd drop in. He taught me a neat trick for clearing the mind and the sinuses, which I forgo to describe here.

And there was a fascinating floating population of wonderful misfits of every description guzzling black coffee, arguing and carrying on every night. It was so much better than high school. I was there every night, taking it all in.

Maxie, the owner, was almost never present. The manager, host, guiding spirit, and resident philosopher was William Lloyd Floyd, an impressive character with a bald head and a flowing moustache and beard. Bill organized debates, acted as master of ceremonies and interlocutor for the semiformal speeches, and answered all questions.

A friend of Bill's had the following conversation with him:

"Bill, you know, you can't go on like this forever."

"Go on like how?"

"Being a beatnik, staying up all night. Not having a real job. Not having any money. You've got a wife. You've got a young child. You really have to do something."

"Do something? Do? What should I do?"

"Sell out, Bill."

"Sell out?"

"Sure, Bill. Sell out."

"You think I should?"

"I think it's the only thing to do."

So the next day, Bill dug out his decent suit, borrowed a white shirt, and a necktie, and went down to LaSalle Street, the Chicago equivalent of Wall Street.

All day he walked up and down the pavement, calling, "I'm selling out! Selling out here! Hey, selling out! Whaddya say, I'm selling out! Selling out, how about it?"

That night he was back in the bookstore.

"I went down there to sell out," he said. "But nobody was buying."

᎙ ᎙ ᎙

I APPEAR to have some kind of mental disorder (that is to say, one I hadn't noticed before). I have always had highly complicated dreams, which frequently take the form of motion pictures. I don't know of anyone else who has dreams with opening and closing credits, and where appropriate, English subtitles.

I've always enjoyed dreaming, have had exciting and stimulating nightmares, erotic dreams that never cross the boundaries of good taste, and one dream which I believe to have been superior to the film *Taras Bulba*, with Tony Curtis.

Lately I've been having dreams that are appallingly boring. I had a long bout of flu last winter, and ever since, there's been something wrong with my projection equipment. Maybe a lingering virus, or a B-vitamin deficiency—or surplus. Whatever the cause, I've been dreaming European Neo-Realist movies like those of Visconti and De Sica, which I can't stand, with occasional excursions into psychological dramas similar to the work of Ingmar Bergman. I dread the emergence of simulated Woody Allen homages to Bergman which I've avoided seeing, but am afraid I may be able to imagine.

I am aware of these dream-screenings being dreams, and while dreaming them, comment constantly that in my waking life I'd never sit through this stuff. I try to shake them off, wake up and growl, grumble, drink water, and then fall asleep again to their unbearable continuing.

I've also had a recurrent dream in which I live in a neo-Tudor house in a place like Westchester County, furnished with antiques, have a wife other than Jill, grown children who are university graduates with good jobs, and friends who drop in for cocktails, mostly professional people. There's a garden outside, and a late model car, dark blue, a Mercedes or a Lincoln. Sometimes I see my hands, poking out of tweed sleeves, open a closet and take out a set of golf clubs. Then I wake up screaming.

This has been going on for months. Between the black-

and-white films and the suburban life scenes, I can only conclude that *I'm having someone else's dreams*!

I tell all this in the hope that some kindly professional, a psychiatrist or a film historian, reading this may have some suggestions.

And especially, if there's a stockbroker in Scarsdale reading, a former member of the Columbia University Film Society, who's suddenly begun having dreams about making his way through a dangerous jungle with a beautiful redhead wearing a bikini made of animal skins—get in touch with me at once! There's something we need to discuss.

🦋 🦋 🦋

RECENTLY I attended a literary soiree. It was meet-the-authors night at the bookstore in the mall. All the writers in the county were there: the flying saucer man, the lady who writes mysteries, the chef who wrote the cookbook, a couple who wrote a book about refinishing furniture, and a novelist who writes about the seamy side of life in Poughkeepsie.

As each of us authors arrived we were given a card, covered with plastic, to pin on. The card had the author's name and the title of his or her book.

Then we all stood around, drinking cider and munching cookies and talking to members of the public, and autographing books. I did fairly brisk business. I must have signed twenty books, the royalties on which would more than cover the tacos I had eaten at the other end of the mall before walking over to join the literati.

The people were nice. The cider was cold. I had a pretty good time. One family was particularly pleasant—an academic-looking mother and father, a middle-size kid, maybe ten, and a little kid, a girl, eight years old tops. They talked about *The Worms of Kukumlima,* a book of mine, long out of print—which didn't do well because primary school teachers and librarians were unable to pronounce the word "Kukumlima" in the title. This bunch was able to say it.

About an hour passed. My admirers began to thin out. Then there was this tiny person standing before me. It was the little kid from the well-spoken family.

"You again!" I said.

"I came to say good-bye," she said.

"That's very nice of you," I said. "Good-bye."

The kid stood there. She had a complicated expression. It was clear something was eluding me.

"No," she said. "You see. . . ."

She started to reach a hand out and then withdrew it. I took her hand.

"You see . . . you're my favorite author."

She stared up at me. *Now* did I understand that this was not an ordinary moment?

"That's very very pleasant to hear," I told her. "You know, I've written about fifty books. I'll bet there are some you haven't found yet."

"I've read thirty-five," she said.

"Really? Thirty-five? Are you sure?"

She reeled off the titles of a dozen or so of the novels, the harder ones.

"You know," I told her, "it's an honor to have a reader like you."

With that she spun on her heel and ran out of the bookstore.

It *is* an honor to have readers like that. And patient! Look how she guided me through that conversation.

❧ ❧ ❧

I GUESS by this time I'm a professional broadcaster, in a small way. It's a lot of fun, and as a lifelong radio fan, I get a kick out of being a participant.

WAMC in Albany, New York, my local public radio station, is real good. I listen all the time, and once I sent in a bunch of short tapes to be used in fund-raising. Then I forgot about it.

So there I am shaving, and the bathroom radio is on.

"Hi, there," I hear a voice say.

"What fool is this?" I think.

"This is Daniel Pinkwater," the voice says.

"Oh. That fool."

I also listen to WAMC when I go for my daily walk. Every morning, my dog Jacques and I do a mile or two at the Vanderbilt Mansion National Historic Site, a beautiful spot.

I have a little headset radio, and I listen to the morning classical music show. The disc jockey is sort of an institution in the Northeast, a guy by the name of Robert J. Lurtsema. Lurtsema is . . . one . . . . of . . . . . these . . . . . slow . . . . talkers. He plays good music, and he . . . takes . . . his . . . . time.

An acquired taste, but I like him all right. On one occasion, he was making an announcement about local musical events—the program comes out of Boston.

So he's saying something like, "Tonight . . . at . . . . Nussbaum Hall . . . the . . . Apollonian . . . String . . . Quartet . . . will perform . . . a . . . new . . . . . work by . . . . composer . . . . Daniel . . . . . Pink . . . . ham."

Well, between "Pink" and "ham," I had a panic attack. "My God!" I thought. "I forgot all about it! I haven't written a note! The Apollonian String Quartet is going to show up and there won't be any music on the stands! Maybe if I write real fast and send it by Federal Express!''

I was halfway to my car when I remembered that I don't write music, and besides, he was talking about some other guy.

It's the power of the medium, friends.

❦ ❦ ❦

I GET wonderful mail. Today I heard from a family in New Mexico. Their kids like a book of mine called *Tooth Gnasher Superflash*. It's about a magical blue car.

What moved the mother of the family to write was the fact that their new U.S./Japanese hybrid looks a lot like the car I drew for the book—same color too. The kids insist it's a real Tooth Gnasher Superflash.

Pleasant enough—routine stuff. But they also sent a picture. It shows the shiny new car. Lined up in front of it are Sara, with her lunchbox and backpack, Tristan, a deliriously happy two-year-old, twisting the leg of his Gumby doll . . . and Goonda, the family pet . . . a turkey.

I wish you could see this picture. A desert landscape, extending to the horizon, the blue car, and kids, and Goonda.

Goonda's lined up perfectly with the kids. He's gazing into the camera. He's looking good, too. His feathers gleam. The car should have a finish like that turkey.

Right after the picture was snapped, I imagine, Mommy cranked up the car and drove Sara to school. Tristan and the turkey must have gone along for the ride.

This is why I am so good-natured. This is why I am so happy. This is the thing I was never able to explain to my boring relations. It's next to impossible to get rich writing children's books, but if you do a good job, you receive the goodwill of many fine Americans . . . and their children . . . . and their turkeys.

☣ ☣ ☣

I RECEIVED a phone call from a woman I know who is *a writer*. She was always going to be a writer. Never wanted to be anything else. She studied for it in college.

"I'm going crazy," she said. "I'm under so much pressure."

"You are?"

"Oh, it's this novel—this novel! It's driving me crazy."

"You're writing a novel, and it's driving you crazy?"

"Yes, and the pressure is terrible. Photographers are calling me all the time to take my picture, my editor keeps calling, and I have to finish it by July. It's my first novel, and I'm so nervous about it."

"So somebody is going to publish it?"

"Yes. They gave me fifty thousand dollars."

"Somebody paid you fifty thousand dollars, and you didn't even finish writing the book?"

"That's not very much for a first novel. Some people get half a million. Do you think I got screwed?"

"Is this novel anything like the short story you wrote?"

"The story is part of the novel. That's what I showed them when they decided to publish the book."

"But that story is about some woman who's in love with a sensitive poet who lives down by the beach. And then there's a moment of stark realization—and she knows who she really is."

"It's going to be much more grounded in the novel, and the imagery will be richer."

Listen, everybody, this makes me sick. No one has ever

given me fifty thousand dollars for anything! My father didn't give me fifty thousand dollars when he died!

Fifty thousand dollars! And I'm a good writer! I don't write stupid stories about guys who live down by the beach and have stupid women in love with them.

I just wanted to get this off my chest.

Thank you.

※ ※ ※

THE scene is the World Freestyle Poetry Semifinals in William McGonagall Memorial Stadium. It's a huge crowd. Norb, Rat, and Eugen the woolly mammoth are there. The master of ceremonies speaks: Ladeez and Gentlemen! Our next poet, from the Land of the Rising Sun! Former sumo champion and haiku-ist in the heavyweight category! LENNY WATANABE!

Lenny comes out. He's got a plastic pocket protector full of ballpoints. Weighs about 375. The crowd goes wild.

Norb speaks: Lookit! This guy should be good. He's built like a rhino.

And Rat says: Shhh! He's going to recite!

Lenny bows. The cheering dies down. Standing in the spotlight, he reads from a sheet of paper: Poem entitled

> "My Dog."
> My dog all muddy
> But he still my buddy.

The MC: Lenny Watanabe, the Tokyo troubador! Let's hear it for him, poetry fans!

That's an excerpt from *Rhymes of Unreason*, one of the episodes in the comic strip *Norb*. Following Lenny Watanabe is the poet you love to hate, the louse of lyrics, the loony laureate, the worst in verse, the monster of meter, the belligerent bard . . . Mad Dog O'Malley!

The crowd loses control, and almost lays hands on Mad Dog, but Rat insists that Norb help her save him, so Eugen the woolly mammoth runs interference through the crowd and . . . .

But I get carried away. Besides, it's not enough to tell the stories. You really have to see the pictures.

I'll tell you how it started. Tony Auth, a Pulitzer Prize–winning editorial cartoonist and real nice guy, had been hired to do illustrations to go with an article I wrote about building model airplanes. I loved the drawings, and called him up to say so.

"I loved the article," he said. "Let's team up."

We decided to try a comic strip. We also decided that we didn't want to do just any old thing. We wanted to do a masterpiece.

So we talked. Me up here in the Hudson Valley, Tony down in Philadelphia. We talked about things we'd loved as kids, radio programs, *Terry and the Pirates*, *Li'l Abner*, *Pogo*. And the great classics of cartooning, *Krazy Kat*, *Little Nemo*, *Barnaby*.

We found out that, more than admiring and enjoying one another's work, we were aesthetically compatible. We contemplated leaving our wives and getting married, but decided to just do the comic strip and let it go at that.

But what was our strip to be? We mulled. We ruminated. We discussed. It went on for two years.

At one point, Tony began sending me panels from imaginary comic strips, not knowing what the story was or who the characters were—just things straight out of his imagination. In one of them there was a character I recognized! It was an old bearded guy, on the order of a wizard. In books, I'd written a couple of characters a little like him, and I had him in mind for a major role later, when I could see him clearer. And now I was looking at him.

It was Norb. A slightly crochety genius-of-all-trades, scientist, explorer, detective, aviator. This was the guy! Our central character. We both agreed.

Now to create a supporting cast and environment. Norb's house was to be a dignified old pile, a combination of 221B Baker Street and the American Museum of Natural History, full of artifacts, trophies, experiments, and odd pets.

Then, to accompany Norb on his adventures, we supplied Rat, a hip and feisty teenaged girl from next door, and Eugen, the last surviving woolly mammoth, about the size of a Saint Bernard. Once we were rolling, we added Jacobowitz, Norb's manservant, stooge, and bodyguard. A big muscle-bound type with a criminal record and a penchant for serious reading.

And we were off! Writing and drawing these folk was pure joy. Tony and I delighted and surprised each other as we turned out the first story. It was to be a "to be continued" strip, a comic adventure with an archvillain and Norb saving the day. This sort of thing is out of favor these days, but we figured it was due for a comeback.

In a matter of weeks, a major syndicate had picked Norb up. We went to a celebratory meeting in New York, with the syndicate sales force, and lunch in a private room in a restaurant, which, curiously, was dominated by a large portrait of Howard Hughes. The guys from the syndicate seemed very serious, and wore suits. They predicted huge success and money beyond our dreams.

Then, in a week, they'd sold Norb to various newspapers to the tune of a hundred thousand dollars a year—half of which was to be ours, Tony's and mine! And that was just the beginning! What sales would the next week bring? And the next?

Norb hit the papers. And the hate mail started immediately. People hated it! I'm not talking about indifference, or mild dislike. I'm talking about hatred.

"This strip makes me feel stupid," many of the letters

read. "I hate Norb. He's a Know-it-all," others wrote. A fair amount of our fan mail consisted simply of drawings of skulls and crossbones, daggers dripping blood, and open graves.

The mail continued, as well as irate calls to newspapers, and petitions. Soon, papers began to drop the strip. We started in about seventy. I'm not sure how many were running it when we pulled the plug last week—one, I think.

We did get one fan letter. It came from a famous novelist. He said he loved Norb, and wouldn't it be great if the American Public were able to tolerate it?

I'm still not sure what went wrong. The only conclusion I can come to is that not enough novelists read a daily paper anymore.

≥ ≥ ≥

THE Checker car, sadly no longer made, was designed to be a taxicab. It was a hybrid, made from Ford, General Motors, and Chrysler components. The body resembled a 1955 Chevy on steroids. Inside it was cavernous. I once easily put two four-drawer file cabinets into the back seat of mine, and had room for a third—and then there was the trunk.

To make the car safe, the makers of the Checker did not resort to crumple zones, impact-absorbing bumpers, and other niceties of design. They simply made everything twice as thick as it needed to be. The owner of the agency from whom we bought our Checker showed us one that had been whacked at an intersection by a fully loaded lumber truck doing fifty. The occupants walked away. When you were inside that car, you knew you were safe from everything but armor-piercing ammunition.

I found that one tended to drive a Checker in a certain

way. Most of the taxicabs in New York were Checkers, and one found oneself negotiating traffic with the same divine right-of-way of the official hacks. Nothing could hurt you—and dents and scrapes looked normal on a Checker. Other drivers would automatically shrink into themselves and defer when they'd see that lumpy silhouette. And so, the driver of a Checker became a lord of the road, changing lanes clear across avenues, diving into tiny holes in traffic, and engaging in contests of nerve with other Checkers with fenders mere microns apart.

These encounters, these airs and caprices with the official Checkers, the yellow ones with honorable scars and the light on top, required not only cool judgment, but a studied nonchalance, and a rakish smile, such as Errol Flynn might have smiled at the stick of a Spad or Nieuport biplane. It helped to languidly chew a toothpick while nearly clicking door handles with another samurai of the streets.

More than once, at night, while I was stopped for a light, one of my back doors would open and someone would get in, usually an elderly woman. Apparently unfazed by the fact that a couple of big dogs were wandering around the passenger compartment, the intrepid New York taxi user would announce a destination.

So I'd take her there. What the hell, I'm never in a hurry. On our arrival, an argument would ensue when I wouldn't accept payment. One old lady refused to get out until I promised to wait while she darted into a shop and bought me a bag of bagels. They're a proud lot, the old ladies of New York.

When we moved to the country, the Checker came with us, carrying about half as much stuff as the moving van could hold. But once here, it failed to fit into the landscape. I was plagued whenever I drove it by hayseeds asking me what it was. And to tell the truth, it fell victim to my snobbishness. It didn't look right to me, pug-ugly that it was, squatting outside the circa-1805 farmhouse. So I sold it cheap, to my friend Steve, who took the old bus back to Hoboken where it belonged.

※ ※ ※

My Maine Coon cat, Zoe, was an easy-maintenance cat. Zoe had never figured out how to get onto furniture. She lived exclusively at floor level.

Every day, I'd dump some food in her dish, and make sure she had fresh water. I kept her litter box clean—and that was it.

Two or three times a day, she'd come to get her head scratched. The rest of the time, she'd sleep or look out the window.

I liked her. I'm pretty sure she liked me. She was nice-looking, and no trouble. For most of the time I had her, I hung out with women who were similar.

I did not marry one of those women. I married someone who was more than nice-looking, and plenty of trouble. Jill had a cat of her own, and when we all moved in together, war broke out. Zoe hated Jill's cat. Jill's cat hated Zoe.

It put a strain on the marriage. Each of us blamed the other person's cat—and by extension, the other person.

Finally, we agreed to give both cats away. We found them homes. Tension abated—somewhat.

We'd been married in the fall. Jill was teaching, and we had deferred our honeymoon. We planned to go to Paris for ten days during Christmas vacation. We never went. Instead, we both came down with flu.

There we were. Sick. Outside, snow and Christmas and city life. Inside, Kleenexes, aspirins, sneezes, and coughs. Jill said the worst part was not having a cat to keep her company while she suffered. Apparently a big, fat, almost brand-new husband was not enough.

We had lots of money—traveler's checks we weren't going to use, plus our refund from the airline. When we felt well enough to go out, we went straight to Aristo-Katz, a posh establishment on the East Side, where we purchased a pure-bred kitten, an Abyssinian.

This is what we got for our $275: the kitten, a bright-eyed darling, two weeks supply of special Aristo-Katz frozen cat food, a comb, a brush, an approved Aristo-Katz cat toy, and an LP record explaining at great length and in incredible detail how to care for our new kitten. We were told how seemingly minor or inadvertent errors in behavior or attitude on our part might scar the kitten psychically for life.

The record explained that one could continue to purchase the special Aristo-Katz food, at prices similar to takeout dinners from a two-star restaurant, or we could concoct it ourselves—a foul-smelling mush the main ingredient of which was fresh kidneys. It also had egg whites, parboiled buckwheat groats, Aristo-Katz vitamin powder, and I forget what else.

We fed Sadie, our Abyssinian kitten, the Aristo-Katz kidney mush, and followed the diabolically complicated kitten rearing instructions for a number of weeks. Then we got tired of the whole business, and began buying commercial cat food at the supermarket.

Sadie seemed to like the stuff in the cans, continued to grow, looked healthy, and the horrible flatulence went away.

Gradually, we began to treat Sadie more and more like a regular pet cat. And she was a wonderful one. Abyssinians are active and athletic. They move with grace and abandon—and are clowns at the same time. Sadie made us laugh a lot. She was the first in a series of Abyssinians we've enjoyed—and the only one that cost us a nickel. In fact, there's a new Abyssinian just come to live with us— but that's another story. I'll tell it another time.

❧ ❧ ❧

SADIE, our first Abyssinian cat, came from a fancy-dancy cat boutique, and cost a relative fortune. Sadie Two, who came along after the first Sadie died, looked and acted like an Abby, but, being of uncertain ancestry, was a bargain at the local pound—free, in fact. In time, she was succeeded by Sadie Three, from the same shelter, a remarkable cat.

Sadie Three had a lovely and distinctive Abyssinian face. For the rest, she looked like the work of an inept taxidermist. Her head had a squashed appearance, and didn't go with her body. Some of her whiskers had a corkscrew curl, and she walked with a strange swaggering gait. Sadie also had a multitude of toes—more than the regulation number. She had a frightening rumble in one lung, and after a time was diagnosed as having feline leukemia. With all this, she lived nine years.

And during those nine years, not a rat, not a mouse, not a vole, not a mole stood a chance anywhere on this farm. Sadie had come to us as a barn cat, and divided her time between the house and her duties extirpating vermin.

Summertime, we might see her one day in three putting in an appearance as a housecat, for the sake of form. The rest of the time, she was in the barn and fields, dealing death to the rodent.

She had no use for other cats except in winter for warmth, although she often preferred to pick out one of the dogs, approach it, stand on its hind legs, her forepaws against its shoulder, and shove it over onto its side, after which she would curl up on the recumbent pooch for a warm nap. The dogs appeared to adore her, and would do whatever she wanted.

She disliked being stroked or held, but occasionally she would leap up onto my shoulder and ride there for a while—an honor for me. She was wraith-thin, weighing no more than five pounds for most of her life.

My wife, Jill, was her favorite, and Sadie would appear instantly, bounding across the fields when Jill called her—and she loved to accompany Jill on walks.

She was a cat with dignity and style, and she died that way. We've had quite a few pets and have attended a fair number of deaths. Hers was unlike any other. Instead of fading away, Sadie, in her final illness, grew more alert as she grew weaker. She appeared to be preternaturally interested in everything that was going on. Just before the end, she dragged herself to the door and insisted on being let out. She spent a day visiting her old haunts, and came back to the house exhausted.

When she came to the actual dying, she gave a cry neither frightened, nor plaintive, nor pained. It was her version of a lion's roar. Conscious and defiant, the cry of a mighty hunter. Her last expenditure of vital force. Then she was gone—Jill and I both felt it—although that remarkable heart continued to beat for another hour or so. We should all die that well.

There were the usual formalities. Jill planted her in the garden next to her favorite sunning rock, and put in some nice flowers. And the inevitable discussion. Were we going to hunt up a Sadie Four?

We would be on the lookout for another Abyssinian cross, but we thought it was time to retire the name. Come summer, when there are lots of kittens at the pound, we'd look for a suitable kitten.

We didn't have to. A few days later, during a rainstorm, there turned up in our barnyard a young cat—unmistakable Abyssinian ancestry. A squashed-looking head. Twenty-four toes. Looks like the work of an amateur taxidermist. And Sadie's very face.

A male this time. We're calling him Augie. He's a good sort. Very robust and affectionate. The other animals like him.

I have no explanation for this. It happened once before, when Arctic Flake, a malamute bearing a strong resemblance to our departed Arnold, showed up. Of course, Augie bears more than a strong resemblance to Sadie. The identical markings and the supernumerary digits put this occurrence in the realm of mystery.

It may be something about Jill that causes these things to happen. They never happened to me before I met her.

I suppose after I die some fat bum will turn up in the yard. Jill will take him by the hand, lead him into the house, and sit him down in front of the computer.

"I don't know, lady."

"Just try to write a story."

"I-I don't know."

"Just try. The dictionary's over here. I'll go and make some pot roast."

I hope the guy likes animals.

☙ ☙ ☙

THERE'S a type of restaurant that always has old movie posters on the walls, and car radiators, horse collars—and other stuff that normally accumulates in garages and barns. And they always have imitation stained glass Tiffany lamps over the tables.

I was eating in one of those places recently, when the big white bulb in one of the fixtures, looking like an ostrich egg, exploded all over a customer. The thing just went to pieces and shed splinters on this guy.

The manager came over, as the customer was picking glass off his clothing.

"Light seems to have exploded," the customer said.

"That's all right," the manager said. "Don't worry about it."

"Thanks," the customer said. He left a tip, picked up his check, and made to head for the cashier's station.

"You're not upset?" I asked him.

"No, I was nearly finished," he said.

To the manager, I said, "Aren't you going to apologize to the guy, or offer to buy him lunch?"

"Why should I? I didn't make the lamp blow up."

More recently a national pizza chain opened a branch in my town. This outfit specializes in deep-dish Chicago-style pizza—which, incidentally, I never encountered when I lived there—but they also offer the traditional thin-crust style.

I ordered the thin crust. In five minutes there it was. Inedible. This stuff was ghastly. You know those Uneeda biscuits? They're like double-thick saltines with plaster of paris? That's what the thin crust was like.

The manager came over. "How's the pizza?"

"It's shocking. It tastes like the thing the pizza is usually delivered on."

"Yes, well, to tell the truth, I wondered why you ordered it. It is pretty nasty. Only four percent of our customers ever have it."

"Then why bother with it—or at the very least, why not warn people about it?"

"Hey, I'm only the manager. It's policy."

This puts me in mind of all those news stories about how Russians are coming over here to learn about management and service, and the American way of doing things. The Russian trainees say that in a few years they'll be just like us. It's my contention that they already are.

❧ ❧ ❧

HOBOKEN provided easy access to wilderness. It was easy to keep a car there, compared to Manhattan. Highways and parkways leading to God's country were only minutes away. Little more than an hour up the Palisades Parkway or the Taconic were magnificent state parks where I'd camp—sometimes driving up on a summer night just to sleep in comparative cool and escape the mosquitoes.

This activity led to serious perusal of the outdoors magazines, and catalogs, acquisition of mountains of survival gear—and ultimately, a familiarity with, and love for, Maine, the mecca of the outdoor types.

Last fall, Jill and I got a free trip to Maine. Some librarians up there wanted to hear me talk, and they offered us a sum of money, two nights in a hotel, and a rented car to get there in.

Naturally, we said yes. The rent-a-car people came through magnificently. They gave us a brand-new European luxury car. Dark blue. Smooth. Fast. Across Massachusetts we went, and then north.

It had been fifteen years since we were in Maine. Last time, we rented a cabin on Moosehead Lake, hiked in the woods, fooled around in a canoe. When we'd had enough of that, we drove down the coast, stopping in little villages, sucking up salt air, scenery, and seafood.

This time we got to Portland, I did my job at the librarians' conference, and we took off with money in our pockets and a full tank of gas.

One of the things you used to do when you went to Maine was stop in at Bean's store. L. L. Bean, famous for the catalog, was open twenty-four hours a day, 365 days a

year. What you'd do was go there at two in the morning—
just to see that it was actually open. Sure enough, the big
old wooden building would have lights on. There would
always be some beat-up old station wagons outside, full of
Labrador retrievers, bedrolls, and shotguns. Inside would
be guys in those red-and-black plaid shirts and hunting
boots, picking up some pipe tobacco and a couple of otter
traps before going up-country.

And we'd wander around, looking at the snowshoes,
and fishing tackle, and industrial grade parkas—maybe
buy a bottle of insect repellent, and some bulletproof socks.
Once I got a Maine woodsman's jacket there with about
fifty-two pockets, and a hood that folded into the collar.

Naturally, we stopped at Bean's on our recent trip. But
it's changed! The outside isn't clapboard any more, it's a
trendy packing-box look with the boards running diag-
onally. The inside has somehow been made vast—larger
than the exterior. The creaky wooden floors and the stairs
with the rubber treads are gone. It's terrazzo now, and
floating staircases with padded leather handrails. There's
an indoor trout pond, and the latest thing in upscale merchandise displays.

And everywhere yuppies. Preppies. Yuppie preppies.
Preppie yuppies. They're squelching around in their
name-brand boating shoes, wearing their little khaki
shorts, their little soft shirts. They're draped all over the
landscaped terraces in front of the store. They're standing
around the giant Ben and Jerry's ice cream stand. And up
and down the main street of Freeport, Maine—one classy
designer outlet store after another. A Disneyland for compulsive shoppers.

Inside the store, they're trying on imported tennis shoes,
acquiring more of those khaki shorts, flowered sweaters,
and the other quaint traditional garments of their class.
The charge-card machines are never silent.

It's a shrine. It's the Santiago de Campostela for people

who went to Andover and Miss Porter's, or want to look as though they had.

Used to be when I visited Bean's I'd feel like Ernest Hemingway. Now we felt like Biff and Buffy.

We had trouble picking out our rented deluxe Euro-yup sedan in the parking lot. I don't have to tell you that we didn't see a single pickup truck with a bird-dog in it.

Shaking our heads, we took off, up the coast, looking for a spot where we could face off with a lobster in dignified surroundings. Looking for the real Maine.

We found it. It's still there. You just have to drive a little longer to get there.

❧ ❧ ❧

SOMEONE'S been selling a kit that purports to train your cat to use the toilet. I know nothing about the product, and simply ask the obvious question—who'd want to share the toilet with a cat?

Years ago an ad used to appear from time to time in the classifieds of a famous counter-culture weekly newspaper in New York. It read: "Train your cat to use the toilet. Instructions one dollar. Thunderbird Cat Service." Followed by a post-office box number.

I noted the ad when it appeared, and asked the obvious question. I'm told that some cats do, of their own volition, use the toilet instead of their little litter boxes. If I had one like that, I'd be willing to pay for instructions to train it to leave alone those facilities designed for humans.

So it happened that I was guzzling cappucino one evening, back in the sixties, with a pleasant young woman I'd just met. At one point she mentioned that she needed money, and thought she'd revive the Thunderbird Cat Service.

"Wait a minute! *You're* the Thunderbird Cat Service?"

"Yes."

"Train your cat to use the toilet? I've always wondered. Tell me about it."

"Well there's not much to tell," she said. "Whenever I'm short of cash, I just have five hundred sheets of instructions printed up, and place an ad."

"Yes, but what's the method?"

"Well you get strainers of various sizes, and fill them with cat sand. Then you suspend them over the toilet bowl, beginning with the largest one. After a few days, you replace it with a smaller one, and then a smaller one. The cat learns to balance on the rim, and aim for an ever-smaller target. Finally you take away the last, and smallest, strainer, and you've got him reconditioned."

"And it works?" I asked her.

"*My* cat uses the toilet," she said. "Then again, he always did."

Years later I knew another woman who had sent in her dollar to the Thunderbird Cat Service, and followed the instructions. They did work up to a point. Her cat, a large black Persian named Bela Lugosi, did abandon the litter box but did not use the toilet. He used the bathtub. Once reconditioned, he stayed that way.

Bela Lugosi was an apt name for the cat. He put me in mind of all those movies in which one of the characters says, "There are some things man was not meant to tamper with."

My sentiments exactly.

❧ ❧ ❧

THIS is going to be about egg creams, and thus requires the obligatory remarks about what an egg cream is. I personally have heard this topic discussed on the radio a thousand times, but there's no way to mention an egg cream without first telling the ninety-nine-point-nine percent of Americans who have never encountered one, and probably wouldn't be impressed if they did, just what is it, an egg cream.

It's an ice-cream soda without the ice cream. Syrup— usually chocolate—a little milk, and soda water. That's it. It has the look and consistency of dirty dishwater, virtually no nutritional content, and a taste like thin air. It has neither egg nor cream.

It is taken very seriously in parts of Brooklyn and the Bronx.

Get any native of the five boroughs of New York City started on the subject, and you'll hear a prose poem. Get natives of any two boroughs of New York talking egg creams, and you'll see a war.

There have been killings in the streets of Brooklyn and the lower East Side of Manhattan precipitated by disputes about the relative virtues of Hershey's versus Fox's U-Bet chocolate syrup.

New Yorkers, said to be people in a hurry, will spend hours arguing about the order in which these ingredients are put together.

Here's the straight goods, supplied by my wife, an actual native of the Bronx: milk in first. Then in goes the syrup. You'll see it kind of plop to the bottom through the milk. Then put the seltzer in, and stir, so in addition to the foam you would ordinarily get, you get extra foam because you're stirring it. Sort of let that drip off, and you've got an egg cream with a lovely head on it.

I've heard her get in fights with outlanders from Brooklyn who believe in putting the syrup in first.

The proportions depend on which candy store you frequented when you were a kid. The one I remember was in Chicago, and offered cherry Cokes, various tooth-rotting penny candy, and was where you could bet on the daily number. Egg creams were unknown.

I sit it out when New Yorkers babble nostalgically and argue about egg creams.

This is not to say that I won't drink one. I've lived in and around the urban East for a long time. They aren't bad. There are things they go with—like a street pretzel. On a hot day, an egg cream can be refreshing. By my lights, a good egg cream is one in which the seltzer is sort of cold.

I associate them with Jewish, or possibly Italian, New York. But once I ordered one in a traditional candy store in the deepest Bronx, and the Hispanic proprietor asked me where I had developed a taste for this Puerto Rican specialty. As successive ethnic groups acquire the candy store, they make its offerings their own, and this guy thought it was something his parents had brought from their island. By now, I'm sure there are East Indians and Koreans who believe their grandmothers in Bombay and Seoul made egg creams. Maybe they did. For all I know, Polynesians may have brought the egg cream from Tahiti to the west coast of South America. It might be a universal manifestation of all cultures. It could be that the nectar gods drank on Olympus, or the mead of Valhalla, was actually egg creams.

If that's so, I'm glad most of us—natives of Brooklyn excepted—have moved on from the age of myth.

It's a whole lot of trouble just to get a chocolate-flavored burp.

※ ※ ※

THE first time I went to Africa, Ken Kelman looked after my loft while I was gone. Considering the condition I found the place in, it seemed the safest thing to do when I wanted to go again was invite him to go with me.

When he agreed, the first thought to cross my mind was that, uncomfortable as he was anywhere outside New York City, let alone in a wilderness, I might be able to get a cheap victory off him in a game of chess—something I had been unable to do for years.

Soon, we were in the Serengeti with our guide, Hassan. Hassan gave good value—we were the first ones out of camp and the last ones back, having seen more and rarer fauna than anyone else—whether we felt like it or not.

This particular day, Hassan had decided to show us leopards. Leopards are elusive and seldom seen. Hassan located every leopard in the district—big and small, active and indolent, plain and fancy. We had taken all the pictures anyone could want of leopard rumps hanging over branches, leopards sleeping, leopards snuffling up gory hunks of gazelle. We didn't care if we never saw another leopard.

When Hassan saw another leopard. "Ooooh! Lookit, bosses! A good one!"

Hassan veered off the bumpy track, and we crashed overland toward the tree with the leopard in it. And crash we did. The front end of the Volkswagen bus disappeared into a deep hole, the windshield pressed against thick grass. The rear end of the bus was up in the air, the wheels spinning. Through the open roof of the bus I saw the leopard drop out of his tree and begin a clockwise circle around us. This was consistent with what I'd been told leopards do when they are annoyed. They come around behind you and tear out your heart.

We made various attempts to pry the bus out. Nothing worked, of course. We were stuck—headfirst in a hole, and we weren't getting out.

Hassan took command. "You tourists stay here. I will go for help."

We were at least eight miles from camp. Night would fall

in a matter of minutes. "Wait a minute!" Kelman and I said, but Hassan was gone.

Now, in the gathering gloom, I am sitting with Ken Kelman in the disabled minibus.

"How long do you suppose we'll be here?" Kelman asks.

"Well, given the probability that Hassan will get lost, and something will drag him away and eat him, I'd say maybe four days before they miss us and come looking."

"That sounds reasonable," Kelman says. "How about a game of chess before the light goes?"

It turned out that *I* couldn't concentrate. Kelman, who had complained the night before that the sound of moths kept him from sleeping, beat me handily.

It got to be good and dark. Being right *in* the bush, as opposed to camp, the African night was very different—some kind of big animal was stomping around *right next* to the bus, even jostling it. In addition to the crunching of underbrush and heavy footfalls, there were piercing cries, grunts, and shrieks.

To make matters unbearable, Kelman appeared to be completely content. Happy even. "You sure played a lousy game," he said. "You mustn't have been paying attention."

By and by we heard shouting and saw lights. Hassan had encountered a bunch of Sikhs in a Land Rover. The Sikhs pulled us out of the hole, and followed us back to camp, where supper was waiting.

There was lots of hooting and hollering as Hassan, Kelman, and I ate our supper. Hassan was telling over and over how he had tried to flag down a lion, mistaking it in the darkness for a man on a bicycle. Presumably the lion was somewhere else now, telling the same story.

Kelman and I were incidental—simply proofs of Hassan's adventure. "And before we crashed, we saw so many leopards! Ask the white men—they were there. Didn't we find a lot of leopards, bosses?"

We confirmed every detail of Hassan's story—even the lies—even the part where he had us begging him to save us.

Kelman and I stole away from the happy scene in the dining tent, promising ourselves that if another opportunity to face danger presented itself, we were going to grab it.

❦ ❦ ❦

HANGING on my wall is a small black-and-white woodblock print I picked up in a junk shop in Poughkeepsie for a few dollars. The artist is named Shiko Munakata. Many years before, I had gotten hold of a little book about Munakata, with many reproductions of his work. I found it in one of those Japanese gift shops.

This was at a time when I was just getting started as an art student, and had even made a few woodblock prints myself. All the woodcuts I'd seen so far had a junky arts-and-crafts quality—and so did mine. Munakata's were different. They were bold and simple, and sprightly and inventive. They had an immediate quality, more like brush drawing than pictures laboriously chipped out of a block of wood.

The text described Munakata's method of working. Instead of making a drawing and carefully transferring it to the wood, he would simply paint the entire surface of the block black, and cut his design directly, carving and drawing in one step.

I tried it. It was fun, and the results were satisfying. I studied the book constantly, trying to figure out how he did things, and why.

I continued working from the hints I was able to extrapolate from the text in my Munakata book. The art teachers at St. Leon's were an inadequate lot, and I imagined that he was my teacher.

I once hitchhiked to New York City because I'd heard that a short subject accompanying a Japanese film had a five-minute segment showing Munakata at work. I sat through the movie twice to see him, nearsighted, swarming over the woodblock like a fat spider, making the chips fly.

Now I saw that he worked so fast that there was no time to think—maybe that was how he was able to impart that spontaneous quality to the prints. I did the same thing, turning out prints in great numbers. I took to carrying small blocks of wood in my coat pockets along with a couple of chisels, and I'd carve woodblocks of people and landscapes directly, as if I were drawing on paper.

I read that Munakata had made some big woodcuts by carving a number of separate panels that fitted together, so I made one, five by seven feet, and glued the resulting prints onto a big sheet of muslin.

By this time, I thought about Munakata all the time. Often I would ask myself, "What would Munakata do in a case like this?" even when the situation had nothing to do with art. I regarded him as my teacher—but the idea of meeting him, or even writing him a letter, or sending him one of my prints, never occurred to me.

Years later, when I was out of school and trying to be an artist in New York, I read in the paper that Munakata was coming to New York. There was to be a big exhibit of his work, and he was going to teach a course at the Brooklyn Museum School. I dove for the phone to register—but while I was dialing, I realized it was too late for that. For better or worse, I'd had my course with Shiko Munakata. He hadn't been present, but that was mere circumstance.

I went to the opening of his exhibit. There he was,

wearing formal kimono and having a good time. I shook hands with him. We also bowed. He also poked my fat belly with an index finger and giggled—and I poked his belly, which was also fat. He didn't speak English, so I wasn't able to tell him that I was his student—but I don't suppose that it mattered.

※ ※ ※

THE Japanese have a tendency to incorporate foreign words without knowing the meaning. They'll use them because they like the way they look or sound. This relates to their use of their own calligraphy as art—I understand the word for writing and painting is the same. So that's why you have that expensive sweatshirt with the words MOONSHOT COW RALPH printed on it.

Some models of the Japanese cars have names at home different from RX-7 and Civic, and Maxima—names like Fellow Max, Sunny Excellent, and Taft.

When I was in Japan I met up with a young woman I'd known in New York. She was sharing an apartment with another English teacher—and they were awaiting a third roommate who was coming over to work for the CIA.

When the third roommate arrived, they explained that they were sharing housekeeping duties, and the new roommate's first chore would be to go out and do the laundry. She hoisted the two full bags onto her shoulders, and went out to look for a clothes-washing establishment.

She was back in half an hour. She'd found a laundromat, handed in the bags, and was given a ticket with which to redeem them the following day. Which she did. The price was amazing, even for 1967 Tokyo—it came to a little over half a buck. The roomies were impressed.

Then they noticed that the garments didn't seem any fresher than they had been. Not washed at all, in fact. The two original roommates followed the new roommate to the establishment. Sure enough, there was the sign: LAUNDROMAT. But what was the place actually? A car park. She had parked the laundry overnight. When she had appeared with the bags of laundry the courteous clerk had simply checked them in, and charged her half the motorcycle rate.

One developed a rare appreciation for the surreal in Japan.

It's hard to understand how people as loony as that are able to cream us in the world market.

♨ ♨ ♨

My brother, who lived in Japan, used to go on a vacation trip to Guam every other year.

"Guam?" I asked him. "What's in Guam?"

"Not a whole lot," he said. "There's a beach, and a bare sort of mountain. You can get some bargains shopping, and there are a couple of fairly decent restaurants."

"It doesn't sound exactly like a fun-seeker's paradise," I said.

"Well, it's cheap," he said. "But the real reason I go there is to renew my driver's license."

"Your driver's license?"

"Guam has the easiest driver's test in the world."

"You go to Guam because of the driver's test?"

"It's a written test, and there are just two questions."

"What are they?"

"Question one is: Do you now have a driver's license? And question two is: How long have you had it?"

"And that's it?"

"Except for the sanity test."

"What's that like?"

"Two questions. One: Are you now sane? And two: How long have you been sane?"

He lived in Tokyo, didn't own a car, and never drove—so I guess it doesn't matter that he gave false answers on the test.

※ ※ ※

ONE of the things that tend to happen in a very old society, like Japan—is that inexplicable traditions live on. For example, my brother, who was a resident alien, had to get a special stamp on his visa every two years. To do this, he had to go to a certain government office building—enter, go down a flight of stairs—to the kitchen—where the head cook would, for a nominal fee, take the stamp out of a cigar box, and stamp his passport. Seems the cook had the stamping concession dating back centuries—and has it still.

My brother had a large gun collection—strictly regulated, as such things are in all countries but ours. But get this—you have to register your guns at the bank. So when my brother received six rifles from overseas, he and I and a Japanese friend had to take them to get registered. Each of us carried two rifles, one on each shoulder, upside-down, the bolts removed, and held in our fingers—walking single-file down the street.

Into a bank! If you ever want to feel totally naked—and freezing cold in the middle of summer, try carrying firearms into a bank.

There was no trouble, of course. The polite Japanese

merely looked away and tried to conceal their amusement at the antics of the crazy Americans.

❉ ❉ ❉

I PICKED this up in a delicatessen. It's a little brochure listing local health and healing alternatives.

Right around here, in what I still think of as a rural area, you can get acupuncture, crystal therapy, movement therapy, reflexology, rebirthing, Zen massage, Hopi massage, Jewish massage, astrology, and there's one guy who does workshops on the Tao of Money.

Some of the practitioners combine different methods. Here's one who does mind-body therapy, reflexology, homeopathy, trance, sacred psychology, and dolphin dreaming.

Here's another one who offers Gestalt therapy, Bodywork, Buddhist therapy, and Metaphysics plus tarot cards.

Plus hot lunch might be something they could add. Or pants pressed. And I notice none of the healers in this directory teaches tap-dancing or gives saxophone lessons. Or haircuts.

I'm thinking there's still some room for innovation in the alternate health and healing business.

I'd take all this even less seriously if a study hadn't been published last week that finds that in New York State (which is the state where I live) twice as many people get killed in hospitals through medical mistakes than are killed by drunk drivers. Seems less likely that something will go drastically wrong during a session of foot-reflexology. Which I might be persuaded to try—especially if I were to get a free oil-change at the same time.

❧ ❧ ❧

WHEN I first moved to the country, I met a fellow named Ned. Ned wanted to give me a bunch of suits. He'd been fat once, it seems, and now he'd gotten thin through an ingenious diet he devised himself.

They were nice suits, and he had a lot of them. I didn't accept any, though.

"I don't want to seem negative, Ned," I told him. "But you ought to hold on to these."

I'd been there myself. I still kick myself for having given away that genuine Harris tweed jacket. A whole family in the Outer Hebrides must have woven a whole winter for that thing to exist—and in my arrogance, I let it go while temporarily svelte.

Ned's diet was fascinating. It was based on his observation that fat people are compulsive and immoderate. Most diets are attempts to make us eat reasonably—and we don't like being reasonable.

Ned figured that if he had to go on a diet, he'd only eat the things he liked best. This is what Ned liked best. He liked bagels. He liked Munster cheese. He liked kosher salami. He liked pears.

So that's all he ate. Salami-and-cheese sandwiches on bagels, and the occasional pear. For two years. He lost about ninety-eight pounds.

"What about a balanced diet?" I asked him. "What about proper nutrition?"

"What could be more nutritious than salami?" he asked me. "As for balance, every day I eat something from the bagel group, something from the cheese group, and something from the pear group. Look at me. Don't I look healthy?"

He looked awful. But who am I to criticize another lunatic?

Every month, Ned would drive a hundred miles to his favorite bagel works in New York, and stock up. He had a huge deep-freeze in which he kept his bagels. His basement was festooned with salamis from Katz's. The Munster cheese and pears he obtained locally.

Once, during a countrywide power failure, I drove over to see him. He was frantically burying sacks of bagels in snowdrifts. His entire hoard was in danger of thawing and going stale.

I lost touch with Ned for a while—and then, one day, ran into him in a store. He was fat again. He was wearing one of the suits.

I looked at him. He looked at me. I wasn't going to bring it up. He did.

"It happened all of a sudden," he said with a shudder. "One morning I woke up and I couldn't look at one of those things."

I've said this before, and I say it again. Bagels can be an enormous power for good or for evil. It is up to us to decide how we will use them.

❧ ❧ ❧

WE developed a surplus of raccoons this past summer. They took to milling around on the front porch, and on one occasion a cat got beaten up badly. We decided to thin them out.

Jill found out that the town animal control officer will lend you a humane trap, and then transport the raccoon to another location where it can make its living.

Our animal control officer is serious and efficient. Her uniform is always crisp, and she does things by the book.

The rules for raccoons specify that they must be liberated in an area with features similar to that in which they were caught, and that area must be within ten miles of their original habitat. The ten-mile rule is to discourage the possible spread of disease.

Jill and the animal officer did a brisk business trapping. It turns out that no raccoon can resist bananas. Marshmallows are also said to be ideal raccoon bait, but Jill refuses to offer empty calories to wildlife. The bananas worked fine.

Morning after morning, we had a raccoon in the trap. The first one was the oldest raccoon anyone had ever seen. He was little, and grizzled, and missing half his nose. Being trapped appeared to make no impression on him. He looked at Jill with indifference, and settled down and went to sleep.

The next raccoon was a big, fat youngster. He was worried. Hadn't finished his banana. He too was loaded into the van and taken off to be released.

After another couple of captures, the animal officer said she needed the trap elsewhere. Jill went out and got her own trap.

Not only did the trapping continue at a lively pace, but the congregations on the porch at night continued. Occasional raccoon fights under our window would make us sit bolt upright in bed. Raccoons are capable of making some extraordinary noises when they're angry or sexually aroused, or competing for bananas.

We began to wonder, just how many raccoons could this place support?

The next night she trapped Half-Nose again.

"The same raccoons are coming back," she said.

Of course they were. We give raccoons the best deal in the county. Where else are they going to get free transportation to the State Park—*and* bananas when they get home?

❉ ❉ ❉

NAVIN Diebold's real name was David Nyvall. He died during the time this book was being written. He did get to read some of the stories in which the Diebold character appears. His comment was "You sure were a lousy printmaker."

In the late 1930s Nyvall was the sabre fencing champion of the State of Illinois. He sported a long waxed moustache, carried a guitar slung over his shoulder, and sang Swedish folk songs at parties. He was a handsome devil, and thought he was hot stuff.

When war broke out, he refused to register for the draft. He also rejected conscientious objector status, saying the idea of war was childish and objecting on religious or philosophical ground would give it too much dignity.

He was duly arrested and taken to the jail in the old courthouse in Chicago. On alternate days he was taken in handcuffs to the courthouse proper and directed to sign up for Selective Service. On the days in between he was beaten in the jail. The local papers pilloried him. He held out for nine months. He was nineteen years old.

When he finally signed, he was immediately inducted to the Army and sent to basic training. His record went with him, and he was kept under close supervision at all times. Each week he was interviewed by an officer who offered to arrange his discharge if he would reveal the name of his Nazi cohorts in Chicago.

Difficult parts of basic training were usually repeated for Nyvall. It would be explained to him that his records had been lost. In the case of the night obstacle course under live machine-gun fire, his records were lost ten times.

Nyvall embarked for Europe as a surgical technician.

The transport he was on was torpedoed and sunk in the Irish Sea, and so was the ship that rescued him. He arrived in England on yet a third troopship in time to participate in the Normandy invasion.

After serving in a field hospital, suturing surgical wounds, during the early part of the invasion, Nyvall received special orders to report to Allied Headquarters in London. He said the telegram was signed "Eisenhower."

Arriving in London he was told that his conduct had been noted beginning with his days in the Cook County jail, and that he was now to be assigned to an espionage unit. He wound up as part of a command group concerned with "audio countermeasures."

Nyvall frequently operated behind enemy lines, his battle dress a hodgepodge composed of elements of Allied and German uniform, armed to the teeth, and carrying no identification. His role, and that of his unit, was to create bogus radio traffic to confuse and disinform the enemy.

During the fighting at Bastogne he was captured by German ski troopers, and escaped, killing two men with a bayonet.

At the end of the war, he took his discharge in Europe and worked for Army Intelligence as a civilian draftsman, sketching newly captured V-2 rockets, the surrendering Wernher von Braun, and other classified booty of war.

When he returned to the States, he attended Cranbrook Academy of Art and began a career as a sculptor in New York.

At some point, and for a number of years, he was a psychiatric patient in V.A. hospitals. Ultimately diagnosed as epileptic, he was discharged from the hospital and lived alone in Chicago.

He regarded the killing of the German soldiers as murder, and it can be argued that for most of the rest of his life he kept himself under virtual house arrest. He had many good friends who visited him, and some patrons who collected his work.

Nyvall had two pupils—me, and sculptor Julian Harr, who said of him, "I don't know if I would have become an artist had I not met Dave, but I do know I learned some of the qualities a decent human being must have to even consider trying to make what some call art—and I call illusion. David was my father, and a friend. I'll miss him."

Same goes for me, brother.

꙳ ꙳ ꙳

AFTER I sold my first children's book—more or less by accident—I got the idea I'd like to do more work like that. So I wrote some more stuff and began making the rounds—and I made a sale! Big publishing house, what counted with me as a healthy advance, and a nice editor.

This editor was not crazy, was helpful, efficient, and friendly. So naturally, she got fired. She called to give me the news, and said, "It's been months since we bought your book. All the editing has been done, your illustrations have been approved, it's been set in type, the cover is designed—in fact, all that has to happen is for the books to be printed and bound. I'm sorry I won't be here to follow through to publication, but don't worry—there's nothing that can go wrong." Thus passed from my life Maria, one of the four or five competent editors I've known out of a round two dozen.

Of course Maria was wrong about there being nothing that could go wrong. A couple of weeks later I received a letter from one Ms. Thornhill at the publishers.

"We regret that we will not be publishing your book

after all," the letter read. "Please return the advance we paid you."

I am known to be a dunce in practical matters, but I have occasional flashes of near-normal intelligence. I wrote Ms. Thornhill the following:

"Enclosed is a letter for you to copy verbatim, sign, and send to me. Best wishes, Daniel Pinkwater."

The letter I enclosed read:

"Big Publisher Inc., regrets that it will be unable to publish your book, and has thus violated its contract with you. We apologize for this. If you will call at our offices, we will return your manuscript and artwork to you. Naturally, all rights to the work are yours, and you may keep any money paid to you so far without obligation to us."

Two days later I received my letter, copied onto the publisher's stationery and signed by Ms. Thornhill.

When I dropped by to pick up my material, it was Ms. Thornhill herself who handed it over.

"Ms. Thornhill," I asked her. "What was the idea of that first letter—the one demanding I pay back the advance?"

"Oh, you'd be surprised," she said, "how many authors don't read their contracts."

I've been shocked any number of times since then by things publishers will do—but I've never been surprised.

I share this little story for the benefit of my fellow writers, especially those who are just starting out. You may want to copy it by hand and keep it in your wallet.

❧ ❧ ❧

JILL and I have been talking about leaving this place and moving to a city. I have no liking for the towns nearby—there are hardly any decent restaurants—and the residents of my adopted valley are generally the least attractive group of people I've encountered. Plus there's nothing resembling a genuine book store. Or bakery.

Sometimes it seems there is no reason to stay here. But there are times, like this morning, when the crows held their morning meeting under my window, I feel I can never leave.

The guy who owned this little farm before we did had one of those psychoses in which the ideas of being an American and killing every living thing in the area are mixed together.

When we first came here, there wasn't a bird or a rabbit in evidence anywhere on the place. Mornings were silent except for the wailing of a few chickens gone wild on the next property—and the crows. When I'd step outside, I'd hear them but never see them.

"There he is, the son of a bitch," they'd say.

Konrad Lorenz writes about this. If you establish a reputation as a crow-killer, every time you show yourself, they'll give out with a warning cry. Thus crows that never knew of your criminal record, and generations of crows yet unborn, will recognize and mark you.

Unfortunately, from a crow's point of view, I present a silhouette not much different from the American rifleman who preceded me. So I was getting tagged with his misdeeds.

What I did about it was reply to the crows in their own language. I have no idea what I was saying, but it tended to crack them up. Still, I never saw a single black feather for the first three or four years.

Now they frolic in plain sight. Some of my crows hang out at the Vanderbilt Mansion National Historic Site, where I take my daily walk. They greet me. Or they acknowledge me, saying something like "Hey! Here comes fatso!" which is anyway not overtly hostile.

At least one of them likes to situate itself as high as possible in a pine tree and imitate a duck and a kitten. It's nothing that would deceive my practiced ear, but it gets a couple of tourists every day in the summer.

It's basically a stupid relationship—mine and the crows—and I doubt they'd miss me if I were gone. But I'm starting to question whether I can just trade it for easy access to fresh bagels.